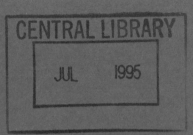

Jewish Humor

By Rabbi Joseph Telushkin

NONFICTION

Nine Questions People Ask About Judaism (with Dennis Prager)
Why the Jews? The Reason for Antisemitism (with Dennis Prager)
*Jewish Literacy: The Most Important Things to Know About the Jewish Religion,
Its People, and Its History*

FICTION

The Unorthodox Murder of Rabbi Wahl
The Final Analysis of Dr. Stark
An Eye for an Eye

Jewish Humor

What the Best Jewish Jokes Say About the Jews

Rabbi Joseph Telushkin

William Morrow and Company, Inc.
New York

It is the policy of William Morrow and Company, Inc., and its imprints and affiliates,
recognizing the importance of preserving what has been written, to print the books we
publish on acid-free paper, and we exert our best efforts to that end.

Telushkin, Joseph, 1948-
    Jewish humor : what the best Jewish jokes say about the Jews / Joseph Telushkin.
        p.   cm.
    Includes bibliographical references and index.
    ISBN 0-688-11027-4
    1. Jewish wit and humor—History and criticism. 2. Jews—Humor—History and
criticism. I. Title.
PN6149.J4T45   1992
809.7'935203924—dc20   92-11966
                                                                                    CIP

Printed in the United States of America

First Edition

1 2 3 4 5 6 7 8 9 10

BOOK DESIGN BY INFIELD DESIGN

For our daughters—
Rebecca
Naomi
and Shira—
who bring so much laughter into my life

Acknowledgments

)

A number of friends and colleagues gave this book a careful reading and made suggestions that strongly improved the manuscript. I am particularly indebted to William Novak, himself the co-author, with Moshe Waldoks, of the classic *The Big Book of Jewish Humor*. Bill graciously called me one day, told me that he had heard I was writing a book on Jewish humor, and that since this was his favorite subject, he would like to see it. I was flattered by his interest and very pleasantly surprised when he sent back eight pages of suggestions based on a careful reading of the manuscript. With the true instincts of a jokesmith, he proposed some alternate renderings that greatly strengthened a number of jokes, and made several very helpful editorial suggestions.

Professor Reuven Kimelman, a noted talmudic scholar and Jewish historian, read the entire manuscript and particularly helped shape the chapter on Jewish jokes about business ethics. In the process, he helped save me from some dangerous overgeneralizations, and I am deeply grateful.

In addition to reading the manuscript and making some very helpful suggestions, Rabbi Jack Riemer sent me a valuable but, alas, unpublished (so far) essay on Jewish humor, which he wrote some twenty years ago.

My good friend, Rabbi Jack Walker, a man who knows more Jewish, and non-Jewish, jokes than anyone I know, not only gave my book the benefit of a careful reading, but also spent hours with me at his Brooklyn home free-associating

7

jokes on every conceivable topic, some of which have inevitably found their way into this book.

My friend and neighbor Rabbi Michael Paley gave the manuscript a careful and very helpful reading. He both challenged and supported my arguments, while telling me a few wonderful jokes I had never heard.

My wife, Dvorah Menashe Telushkin, took time off from her own writing to do a careful line-edit. She prodded me to clarify certain murky passages, and rewrote a number of jokes that I had originally heard from her and had mangled in an earlier draft.

I joyfully acknowledge as well the detailed editorial help of David Szonyi. This is the second book of mine that David has edited—*Jewish Literacy* was the first—and he made thousands (that is not a misprint) of suggestions, the large majority of which I accepted. What more can I say?

It is a pleasure to thank my good friend and agent Richard Pine, who possesses an extraordinary combination of business acumen, literary sensibility, and genuine *menschlikhkeit.*

At William Morrow, I have likewise been blessed with an editor who has become a dear friend, Elisa Petrini. Her critique of my manuscript's first draft was so precise and unarguable that it impelled me to do a great deal of rewriting. Thank God. Since the publication of *Jewish Literacy,* I have come to know a number of other people at William Morrow who have generously extended themselves to me, Skip Dye, Lisa Queen, Michelle Corallo, and Sonia Greenbaum in particular.

While writing this book, I frequently recalled the person from whom I first heard a particular joke. I know I won't remember everyone, but I would like to thank Rabbis Irving "Yitz" Greenberg, Ephraim Buchwald, Leonid Feldman, Levi Weiman-Kelman, Norman Lamm, Hanoch Teller, Joel Wolowelsky, Samuel Dresner, Louis Jacobs, and Pinchas Peli of blessed memory, as well as Judge Nicholas Figueroa, Professor Jacob Milgrom, Dr. Stanley Rosenfeld, Professor Charles Liebman, Dr. Howard Siegel, Ilan Ezrachi, John Silo, Daniel Taub, and Ruth

Wheat. I would also like to thank Beverly Woznica.

Finally, and perhaps most important: I grew up in a household where Jewish jokes were told and appreciated. My father, Solomon Telushkin, of blessed memory, was not generally a joke teller, but my mother, Helen Telushkin, remains a raconteur of note. Indeed, my father used to claim, with a considerable touch of hyperbole, that my mother would destroy the whole world for the sake of a good line. My mother also laughs hard at jokes, and provided an indispensable climate for any budding joke teller. My uncle, Bernie Resnick, of blessed memory, one of the dearest people in my life, also loved Jewish jokes and told them well and often.

And finally, I come to three more people who have enriched my life with laughter, and it is to them that I have dedicated this book.

CONTENTS

▶

Contents

Jewish Humor

Introduction
What Is Jewish About Jewish Humor?

▶

When the first-century Rabbi Hillel was asked by a would-be convert to define the essence of Judaism while standing on one foot, he told the man, "What is hateful unto you, don't do unto your neighbor. The rest is commentary; now go and study." Some two thousand years later, Israeli Rabbi Shlomo Lorincz related Hillel's response to American economist Milton Friedman, then serving as an adviser to the Israeli government, and asked if he could summarize economics in one sentence. "Yes," replied Friedman. "There is no such thing as a free lunch."

Is there one sentence that can capture the essence of Jewish humor? I'm afraid not. How could one statement encompass jokes about Jewish mothers, reckless and rude drivers in Israel, and antisemites? As I hope to make apparent, Jewish humor reveals a great *many* truths about the Jews, but no *one* great truth. Indeed, 150 years of Jewish jokes, and 2,000 years of folklore and witticisms, have the uncanny ability to express truths that sociological or other academic studies usually miss.

A caveat: An analysis of the Jews based on humor and folklore alone necessarily leaves out some important topics. Nothing in these pages reflects Judaism's understanding of God's omnipotence, or why Jews believe they were chosen by God, or the Jewish position on birth control. I would gladly have included these subjects had I found jokes about them, but I didn't.

Many other important topics are the subject of jokes, but not very funny ones. As anyone who has ever perused a book of jokes quickly learns, all too many are not truly funny. I decided early on that it would be cruel (although hardly unusual) punishment of my readers to include such material, merely to have an excuse to say something about the joke's subject.

The good news is that many of the most important issues that Jews think about, often obsessively, *are* expressed in Jewish humor.

Want to know a Jewish reaction to the antisemitic accusation that Jews control world governments and dominate world finance? Well, there is a joke about it (see page 107).

Has Jews' concern with their and their children's financial success caused their values to go awry? This weighty question has been considered in many religious works, but there also is a joke about it, one that is particularly funny and insightful (see page 34).

Are Jews, products of a culture averse to physical violence, disproportionately prone to verbal ferocity and combativeness? Guess what? There's a joke about it, many for that matter (see pages 97–104). Just as there are jokes about Jews who assimilate or who convert to Christianity.

What makes a joke Jewish? Obviously, it must apply to Jews, but more significantly, it must express a Jewish sensibility. Merely giving individuals in a joke Jewish names, or ascribing the joke to Jewish characters, does not a Jewish joke make.*

---

*For example, a recent book containing hundreds of "Jewish" jokes includes the following: "The husband walked into the room and sneered, 'Why are you bothering to iron your bra? You don't have anything to put into it.' ...'I iron your shorts, don't I?' his wife answered."

This is not just a bad Jewish joke—and it's not a Jewish joke at all, but rather a fairly typical, and hostile, American sex joke. It would be equally out of place were it in a book of "great" Irish or Italian jokes.

Jewish sensibility, however, concerns precisely those subjects and values that receive disproportionate attention among
Jews. Antisemitism, financial success, verbal aggression, and assimilation are all particularly significant in Jewish life. Antisemitism, for example, is one of the few issues that unites virtually
all Jews. A large number of American-Jewish organizations are
devoted to exposing and combating antisemitism. Ethnic groups
far larger than the Jews—the Irish and Italian Americans—apparently feel more secure, for they have far fewer "defense"
organizations.

Professional success is highly emphasized and encouraged
in Jewish life. It is no coincidence that Jews have achieved considerable affluence in every society in which they have had
equal rights.[1]

Verbal combativeness and aggression are well-known Jewish characteristics. "Spare me from gentile hands and Jewish
tongues," ran a nineteenth-century Yiddish proverb in Eastern
Europe. "Three Jews, three opinions" (in some versions, "four
opinions," lest one of the Jews be a schizophrenic) is a common American-Jewish cliché. When other arguments fail, members of the Israeli Knesset (parliament) have been known to
accuse their opponents of holding "Nazi-like" views[2]; similar
rhetorical excesses frequently poison American-Jewish life.

Finally, there is assimilation, which in the relatively tolerant
world of America, Jews tend to view as the preeminent threat
to Jewish survival. With intermarriage rates now 50 percent or
higher, countless communal leaders, academics, and other committed Jews warn of the danger of American Jewry "melting
away" into the broader populace.

Jews feel anxiety about all these subjects, and one of the
characteristic ways in which they, and most other people, deal
with their anxieties and fears is by laughing at them: Anything
that can be mocked immediately seems less threatening. The
greater the anxiety a particular subject produces, the more jokes
will be made about it. For example, since most American Jews
today feel quite comfortable among their gentile neighbors, rel-

atively few jokes about antisemitism are being created. But look at collections of Jewish jokes from fifty or sixty years ago, when Jews in this country were far less secure, and you find many jokes ridiculing Jew haters. Among Jews in Russia, however, where antisemitism is still widespread—and was, until recently, government-sponsored—such jokes are more common and are still being created (see pages 117–123).

Other jokes have nothing to do with Jewish anxieties, but reflect the distinctive thought patterns of the Jewish mind. Jokes involving logic and argumentation emanate as directly from the Jewish experience and Jewish creativity as do those about assimilation and verbal aggression. The Talmud, one of the two cornerstone works of Judaism (the other, of course, is the Bible), is frequently concerned with finding logical solutions to seemingly insoluble legal and ritual problems. The most widely studied of its sixty-three tractates, *Bava Mezia,* opens with a legal conundrum: Two men come into court clutching a garment. Each asserts that he was the first to find it; needless to say, there are no witnesses. The Talmud spends pages, and the average yeshiva student dozens of hours, trying to find a logical method for assigning ownership of the garment.[3] Probably no other culture exists in which so many people have concerned themselves with such intricate legal issues. Naturally, takeoffs on the reasoning processes used in talmudic disputes have long since found their way into Jewish humor:

A man, having been caught with another man's wife, is brought before a rabbi.

"You are a vile person," the rabbi tells him.

"Will you condemn me, Rabbi, before you let me prove to you I'm innocent? You admit, don't you, that I am entitled to have sexual relations with my own wife?"

"Of course."

"And you will grant, Rabbi, that the man who accused me is permitted to have sex with his wife?"

"Obviously. What a question!"

"And may that man have sex with my wife?"

"That's disgusting. Of course not."

"Well, then, Rabbi, everything makes sense. You yourself concede that I am permitted to have sex with a woman with whom my accuser is forbidden to have sex. All the more so should I be entitled to have sex with a woman with whom even he is permitted."[4]

Family relationships also are central to Jews. While the family is important in all societies, Jews seem to talk about it more than do members of other groups. That is why the expression "a real Jewish mother" has come to refer to an overly concerned and worried mother of any ethnic or religious background. Novelist Herbert Gold claims that the word "family" follows "Jewish" as inexorably as "cancer" follows "lung."

Of course, the characteristics I have just described are hardly confined to Jews. If they were, Jewish jokes would have little attraction for non-Jews. Yet the long-standing Jewish prominence in American comedy—over the past forty years, some 80 percent of the country's leading comics have been Jews*—suggests that Jewish humor has a broad-based appeal. While the whole constellation of Jewish characteristics described in this book is not found in any other group (or in any one Jew), many non-Jews share one or more Jewish obsessions. Ask Italian Americans if relationships inside Jewish families are any more intense than those inside theirs. Nor, for that matter, do Jews have a monopoly on sharp tongues and argumentative or divisive behavior. Indeed, some jokes regarded as classically Jewish have the annoying habit of showing up in other people's collections of humor. I was amazed to discover the following story,

---

*This estimate is made by Steve Allen, a non-Jewish comedian and historian of American humor (Steve Allen, *Funny People,* p. 30. Note: Full references are not provided for books listed in the Bibliography at the end of this book). "American comedy," Allen believes, "is a sort of Jewish cottage industry" (p. 11). A listing of twenty of the most prominent American-Jewish comedians indicates the disproportionate success of Jews in this area: Woody Allen, Jack Benny, Milton Berle, Fanny Brice, Mel Brooks, Lenny Bruce, George Burns, Sid Caesar, Billy Crystal, Rodney Dangerfield, Danny Kaye, Sam Levenson, Jerry Lewis, Groucho Marx, Jackie Mason, Zero Mostel, Joan Rivers, Mort Sahl, Phil Silvers, and Henny Youngman.

versions of which appear in virtually every major collection of Jewish humor, in Professor Christie Davies's *Welsh Jokes:*

> *A Welshman was shipwrecked at sea and marooned on a desert island. When a passing vehicle picked him up five years later, the crew was amazed to find his little island covered in fine buildings that he had built himself. With pride the Welsh Robinson Crusoe took the captain round the island and pointed out to him his house, workshop, electricity generator, and two chapels.*
>
> *"But what do you need the second chapel for?" asked the captain.*
>
> *"Oh," he replied. "That's the one I don't go to."*

Professor Davies, who presents this story as a typical example of Welsh humor, acknowledges that it is widely told about a shipwrecked Jew as well. But that does not mean that the joke is interchangeable among all ethnic groups. It would not sound plausible, Davies argues, were it told about Swedes, Italians, or the Irish, because the joke depends on the fact that Judaism and Welsh nonconformist Protestantism are religions in which the community is not under the control of one universally acknowledged religious leader, such as a pope. In groups like these, individuals tend to arrogate to themselves the right to make decisions about religious beliefs and practices rather than submit to religious interpretations and discipline imposed by others.[5]

Although the joke's essence and punch line are virtually the same in the Jewish and Welsh versions, there is one important difference. In most Jewish versions, when the man is rescued, all that he has built is a hut and two simple synagogues ("the one where I pray, and the one I wouldn't set foot into"). On the dozens of occasions I have heard this joke told, the marooned Jew never puts up a workshop or constructs an electric generator. Had such details been inserted, the joke would no longer have sounded plausible, because in the Jewish self-image, Jews are lawyers, doctors, accountants, and businessmen, not Robinson Crusoes or Mr. Wizards.

And yet the Welshman's behavior corresponds exactly to what Jews expect of non-Jews. Jackie Mason claims that when a car owned by gentiles breaks down, "in two seconds they're under the car, on top of the car. . . . It becomes an airplane and [the gentile] flies away." But when a Jewish-owned car breaks down, "you always hear the same thing: 'It stopped.' And the husband says: 'I know what it is. It's in the hood.'

"[The wife] says: 'Where's the hood?'

"[And the husband responds]: 'I don't remember.'"[6]

Mason's joke suggests both the wit of ethnic humor and the dangers of negative stereotyping. The most popular segment of his long-running Broadway show, *The World According to Me,* was an extended elaboration of the "differences" between Jews and gentiles: Jews are ambitious, gentiles are plodders; Jews work in business or the professions, gentiles do physical labor ("Did you ever see a [hardhat] on the top of a building yell, 'Happy Passover!'"); Jews eat huge quantities of food, gentiles drink vast quantities of liquor.

Although Jackie Mason's humor has sparked far more laughter than offense, the stereotyping inherent in much ethnic humor is worrisome. Far more often than most joke tellers will acknowledge, some hostile stereotypes are so negative as to do real damage to the ethnic group being mocked. The unrelenting depiction of Poles as idiots in "Polish jokes" has influenced the way many people view Poles, and the way some Polish Americans view themselves. (Imagine the ethnic group to which you belong becoming a synonym for "stupid.") And yet a 1975 study revealed that Polish Americans are the third most affluent ethnic group in the United States, after the Jews and the Japanese.[7] Because of all the negative stereotypes about Poles, many Americans would assume they are underachievers.

The ongoing torrent of "JAP [Jewish-American princess] jokes," which depict all Jewish women as materialistic, bitchy, and sexually frigid, has hurt the image of Jewish women. In fact, more than a few Jewish men justify their preference for gentile girlfriends by claiming that Jewish women are inordinately selfish, cold, and obsessed with acquiring possessions.

Far more disturbing, however, is the fact that the image of Jewish women conveyed in JAP jokes has been used to exonerate a man who murdered a Jewish woman. In 1982 an all-gentile jury in Phoenix, Arizona, sitting in judgment on Steven Steinberg, who had murdered his wife, Elana, was repeatedly told that the term "JAP" described Jewish women who were materialistic, frigid, and nagging, and that Elana Steinberg was such a person. The "JAP defense" was so successful that Steinberg was acquitted and permitted to inherit his wife's property. "The guy shouldn't have been tried," one juror told a reporter. "He should have had a medal."*

In recent years, the very negativism of so much ethnic humor, and the animosity it provokes, have caused many comedians to shy away from ethnic material. Naturally, there is even a Jewish joke about this:

Gold is telling his friend a story: "One day, Cohen and Levine were going—"

"Cohen and Levine, Cohen and Levine," the friend stops him angrily. "Why are your jokes always about Jews? Why don't you tell them about the Chinese for once?"

Gold is taken aback. "You're right," he says. "One day, Soo Lung Mu and Mao Tsu Nu were going to Soo Lung Mu's nephew's Bar Mitzvah. . . ."

*Shirley Frondorf, *Death of a Jewish American Princess: The True Story of a Victim on Trial* (New York: Villard Books, 1988). Sadly, the outrageous verdict in the Steinberg trial has not halted the spread of JAP jokes and other hostile material. Observers have reported the presence of T-shirts on college campuses asking HAVE YOU SLAPPED A JAP TODAY? and a poster of a woman holding a Visa card and can of Tab soda, with the headline BACK OFF BITCH. I'M A JAP BUSTER! At Cornell University, a "humor" magazine published a feature called "JAPS-B-GONE: A Handy Info Packet for the Home Exterminator," with instructions telling readers how to kill a JAP. Letty Cottin Pogrebin notes that "logically, there's no difference between 'Kill a JAP,' and 'Kill a Jew' since women who are called JAPs are also Jews, yet few Jewish people react to JAP 'joking' with anything like the horror and outrage that would accompany the first T-shirt that said HAVE YOU SLAPPED A JEW TODAY? or BACK OFF, YID, I'M A JEWBUSTER" (Pogrebin, *Deborah, Golda, and Me: Being Female and Jewish in America* [New York: Crown Publishers, Inc., 1991], p. 232).

The issue, however, is subtler and more complex than jokes about Bar Mitzvahs, circumcisions, or eating pork suggest. The issue, rather, is, can one tell ethnic jokes without dehumanizing the joke's subject? Pick up any collection of ethnic jokes, and you will find many stigmatizing Italians as mafiosi, Irish as alcoholics, British as uptight and kinky, and Jews as overly sharp in business dealings. And while we might all agree that it's wrong to stereotype a group, it's also true that offensive ethnic jokes usually don't arbitrarily target their victims; often there is a factual basis for the flaws ascribed to different groups. In fact, that's what makes these jokes "familiar" and funny. If the Irish tell many funny stories about alcoholism—in collections of Irish humor, a third or more of the jokes are invariably about drunkenness—that is because, as Nathan Glazer and Daniel Moynihan conclude in *Beyond the Melting Pot,* their classic study of ethnic America: "A dominant social fact of the Irish community is the number of good men who are destroyed by drink." Such jokes continue to be told because the problem has persisted, even with Irish-American upward mobility. "In ways," Glazer and Moynihan have written, "it is worse now than in the past; a stevedore could drink and do his work; a lawyer, a doctor, a legislator cannot."[8]

People who oppose telling ethnic jokes would have us believe that the whole genre is nonsense, that alcoholics, neurotics, oversensitive people, and shady characters are evenly distributed among all groups. However, tolerant as it sounds, this assumption makes no sense, for it implies that history and culture have no impact on human beings. But, of course, they do. What makes Jews Jewish is a specific religious culture and historical experience that has shaped their values and strongly influenced how they view the world.

Part of that religious culture is a proclivity for self-criticism. The biblical prophets repeatedly denounced their fellow Jews for their moral lapses; the Jews reacted, not by hating the prophets, but by canonizing their words and making them part of the Holy Scriptures. This tradition has carried over into Jewish humor, so much so that Sigmund Freud, in his pathbreaking study *Jokes and Their Relation to the Unconscious,* claims that self-critical jokes are one of the distinguishing and characteristic features of Jewish humor. Freud insists, however, that Jews' self-critical jokes are entirely different from those told by antisemites. These acknowledge no good in Jews; in fact, they often deny their very humanity. Only people with a profound animosity toward Jews would tell such a "joke" as "How many Jews fit into a Volkswagen?" "506. Six in the seats, and 500 in the ashtray."[9]

This does not mean, however, that only antisemites joke about the terrible events of Jewish history. During the Hitler era, but before the revelations of the gas chambers, German Jews would tell of two Jews who meet in Cologne. "Can I borrow some cigarette paper?" one asks the other. "Sorry," the second one answers. "I used my last one to wrap up my meat ration."[10]

The challenge confronting the teller of ethnic jokes is to avoid blurring the line that separates insightful, even scathing, humor from so-called jokes that are really an excuse for expressing hostility and prejudice.

While I have yet to find a fully satisfying formula for distinguishing fair from unfair ethnic humor, the following four guidelines should help ethnic storytellers to avoid bloody noses and broken friendships:

1. Would you be willing to tell the joke to a member of the group of whom it makes fun? If not, why?

2. If members of the group discussed in the joke don't find it as funny as or funnier than do outsiders, it's probably hostile and shouldn't be told.

3. The more biting the punch line, the more cautious nonmembers of the group should be before telling it. Years ago, black comic Dick Gregory announced that his son had told him that he no longer believed in Santa Claus: "I don't believe no white man would have the guts to come into our neighborhood

after midnight." Told by a white comic, this joke likely would have crossed the bounds of good taste.

4. Finally, when jokes treat members of an ethnic group not as individuals but *only* as stereotypes (as in Polish jokes or JAP jokes), they become offensive.

A closing confession: Having argued earlier that no one statement can summarize Jewish humor, I herewith present three jokes—one European, one American, and one Israeli—that come as close as any to conveying the contradictions and anxieties that have long characterized many Jews:

> *In the 1920s, a Jew travels from his small Polish shtetl to Warsaw. When he returns, he tells his friend of the wonders he has seen:*
>
> *"I met a Jew who had grown up in a yeshiva and knew large sections of the Talmud by heart. I met a Jew who was an atheist. I met a Jew who owned a large clothing store with many employees, and I met a Jew who was an ardent Communist."*
>
> *"So what's so strange?" the friend asks. "Warsaw is a big city. There must be a million Jews there."*
>
> *"You don't understand," the man answers. "It was the same Jew."*[11]

The "Jew in Warsaw" joke directly confronts the issues that divide the souls of so many Jews. For example, leaders of the intensely Orthodox Lubavitch movement have long noted that a large percentage of their contributors are totally irreligious Jews. As regards American Jewry's political views, it's been said that "Jews earn money like Episcopalians and vote like Puerto Ricans."*

---

*This quip simultaneously confronts some of the opposing stereotypical images non-Jews have about Jews. In the West, one common stereotype of Jews has been that they are leftists, even as newspaper and government propaganda in the Communist world depicted them as capitalists. Studies of non-Jews' attitudes to Jews indicate that the same people often hold conflicting images; those who agree with the statement that "Jews are always trying to push in where they are not wanted" are likely to also believe that "Jews are clannish, always sticking together."

Another reflection on the Jewish psyche:

What's a Jewish telegram?
It reads, "Letter to follow. Start worrying."

And finally, my own favorite story:

A group of elderly, retired men gathers each morning at a café in Tel Aviv. They drink their coffee and sit for hours discussing the world situation. Given the state of the world, their talks usually are depressing. One day, one of the men startles the others by announcing, "You know what? I am an optimist."

The others are shocked, but then one of them notices something fishy. "Wait a minute! If you're an optimist, why do you look so worried?"

"You think it's easy to be an optimist?"

The "distressed optimist" strikes the right chord in much Jewish humor. By insisting that the world is moving toward perfection, and that the messianic days lie in the future, Judaism encourages Jews to be optimists. But Jewish history, with its tragic record of crusades, expulsions, pogroms, and the Holocaust, impels Jews to pessimism. Hence, as Jews, we are optimists—with worried looks on our faces.

1

"Oedipus, Shmedipus, as Long as He Loves His Mother" The Inescapable Hold of the Jewish Family

▶

Between Parents and Children

Three elderly Jewish women are seated on a bench in Miami Beach, each one bragging about how devoted her son is to her.

The first one says: "My son is so devoted that last year for my birthday he gave me an all-expenses-paid cruise around the world. First class."

The second one says: "My son is more devoted. For my seventy-fifth birthday last year, he catered an affair for me. And even gave me money to fly down my good friends from New York."

The third one says: "My son is the most devoted. Three times a week he goes to a psychiatrist. A hundred and twenty dollars an hour he pays him. And what does he speak about the whole time? Me."

The intense connectedness of the Jewish family is no invention of modern Jewish humor. Its roots go back to the fifth of the Ten Commandments: "Honor your father and mother."[1] Today people take it for granted that religion furthers family close-ness; "A family that prays together stays together," a popular catchphrase of the 1950s declared. But, in fact, it was highly unusual to place respect for parents in a religion's most basic legal document. New religions generally try to alienate children from parents, fearing that the elders will try to block their off-spring from adopting a way of life different from their own. In the United States, many religious cults are notorious for loosen-ing, if not shattering, children's familial attachments.*

Hostility to parents also characterizes radical, particularly totalitarian, political movements. Both Nazi and Communist so-cieties instructed children to inform party officials of any anti-government acts or utterances by their parents. In the Soviet Union, well into the 1980s, children who joined the Russian equivalent of the Boy Scouts took an oath to follow in the foot-steps of Pavlick Maroza. During the 1930s, twelve-year-old Pav-lick informed Communist officials of antigovernment comments made by his father, who was summarily executed. Outraged, the boy's uncle killed him. For the next half-century, until Gorba-chev came to power, Pavlick Maroza was held up to Soviet youth as a model citizen, and statues of him were erected in parks throughout the USSR. One can only imagine the discomfort of parents who, taking their children to a park, were asked to ex-plain whom the statue was depicting. "Pavlick Maroza," the father (or mother) would answer. "And what did he do, Daddy?" It must have made for some very unpleasant moments.

It is thus quite striking that from its very beginnings, Judaism

---

*Even Christianity, which has long been very family-oriented, was any-thing but in its earliest days. Jesus declared: "No one can come to me without hating his own father and mother..." (Luke 14:26). In the gospel of Matthew, Jesus advises a young man not to attend his father's funeral, but to follow him instead (8:21–22). Only after Christianity became established was family cohesiveness emphasized.

placed so positive an emphasis on parent-child relations.† Jewish humor, however, is concerned with the down side of this encounter, with what happens when the glorified relationship becomes too intense. Intimations of such an overintensity can be found in the Talmud. Some rabbis placed virtually no limits on filial obligations: "Rabbi Tarfon had a mother for whom, whenever she wished to mount into bed, he would bend down to let her ascend [by stepping on him]; and when she wished to descend, she stepped down upon him. He went and boasted about what he had done in his yeshiva. The others said to him, 'You have not yet reached half the honor [due her]: has she then thrown a purse before you into the sea without your shaming [or getting angry at] her?'" (*Kiddushin* 31b).

As if to ensure that children, no matter how well they treated their parents, would still feel guilty, the Talmud relates the story of a righteous gentile, Dama, who was about to conclude the sale of some jewels from which he would derive a 600,000 gold *denarii* profit. Unfortunately, the key to the case in which the jewels were held was lying beneath his father, and the old man was taking a nap. Dama refused to wake him, "trouble him," in the words of the Talmud. Of this same Dama, the Talmud relates: "[He] was once wearing a gold embroidered silken cloak and sitting among Roman nobles, when his mother came, tore it off from him, struck him on the head, and spat in his face, yet he did not shame her" (*Kiddushin* 31a).

So extreme and unending are the demands some talmudic rabbis make of children that one sage, Rabbi Yochanan, declared in despair, "Happy is he who has never seen his parents" (*Kiddushin* 31b).

In similar fashion, in the story about the three women in

†At a lecture, a questioner once challenged my assertion that early Judaism promoted the parent-child relationship: "Isn't it true that God's first command to Abraham was to leave his father's home?"

"It is true," I answered. "But he was seventy-five at the time [see Genesis 12:4]; he was entitled."

Miami Beach, the best way a son can "honor" his mother is by paying a psychiatrist a fortune to speak about her nonstop.

The linking of psychiatry and Jewish mothers is no coincidence. While Jews are overrepresented in medicine in the United States, in no other specialty is this more the case than in psychiatry (477 percent of what would be normal, given Jewish representation in the general population).*

Large-scale Jewish involvement has characterized psychoanalysis, in particular, since its inception. Sigmund Freud selected C. G. Jung to be the first president of the International Psychoanalytic Association because he did not want psychiatry to be dismissed as a "Jewish science" (which the Nazis did anyway) and Jung was the only non-Jew in Freud's inner circle. "It was only by [Jung's] appearance on the scene," Freud claimed in a letter to a friend, "that psychoanalysis escaped the danger of becoming a Jewish national affair."

Jewish jokes about psychiatry almost invariably involve the family, and they have gone through two phases. In the earliest phase, they dealt with the inability of unsophisticated Eastern European Jews to understand the powerful new insights provided by psychiatry.

A mother is having a very tense relationship with her fourteen-year-old son. Screaming and fighting are constantly going on in the house. She finally brings him to a psychoanalyst. After two sessions, the doctor calls the mother into his office.
"Your son," he tells her, "has an Oedipus complex."
"Oedipus, Shmedipus," the woman answers. "As long as he loves his mother."

More recent humor assumes that modern Jews are sophisticated about psychology. "Every Jew is either in therapy, has just

---

*More than a few people have noted that what goes on in the psychoanalytic encounter is not totally unlike what goes on in the study of Talmud. Unlike most intellectual disciplines, Talmud is not normally studied alone. Traditionally, two Jews struggle together to probe and decipher a talmudic text, just as in analysis a doctor and patient jointly strive to make sense out of what at first seems unfathomable.

finished therapy, is about to enter therapy, or is a therapist," claims a current witticism. Woody Allen, the popular culture's image of the quintessential neurotic Jew, has revealed that he has been in analysis for over twenty years.

Not surprisingly, then, Jewish jokes about psychoanalysis have gone well beyond "Oedipus, Shmedipus":

Goldstein has been in analysis for ten years, seeing his doctor four times a week. Finally, the analyst tells him that they've achieved all their goals, he doesn't have to come back anymore. The man is terrified.

"Doctor," he says, "I've grown very dependent on these meetings. I can't just stop."

The doctor gives Goldstein his home phone number. "If you ever need to," he says, "call me at any time."

Two weeks later, Sunday morning, six A.M., *the phone rings in the doctor's house. It's Goldstein.*

"Doctor," he says, "I just had a terrible nightmare. I dreamed you were my mother, and I woke up in a terrible sweat."

"So what did you do?"

"I analyzed the dream the way you taught me in analysis."

"Yes?"

"Well, I couldn't fall back to sleep. So I went downstairs to have some breakfast."

"What'd you have?"

"Just a cup of coffee."

"You call that a breakfast?"

Jewish parents are also famous (in some circles, infamous) for anxiously hovering over their children. "A Jewish man with parents alive," Philip Roth wrote in *Portnoy's Complaint*, "is a fifteen-year-old boy, and will remain a fifteen-year-old boy until they die." A rabbi I know, who grew up in the intensely Orthodox neighborhood of Borough Park, Brooklyn, told me that it was his wife who taught him that one could express love for one's children by taking pleasure in their personalities. "My parents," he explained, "expressed their love through excessive nervousness and worrying." That was also the case with Mell

Lazarus, creator of the cartoon strip "Momma." Reminiscing about his overly attentive mother at a seminar on Jewish humor, Lazarus recalled, "We had very many interesting conversations, about my posture for example."

The overinvolvement of mothers in their children's lives might well have several roots. The dominant middle-class ideology of the 1940s and 1950s—and Jews were quintessentially middle class—dictated that a father should work, and that the mother stay home with the children. A large number of highly educated Jewish women found themselves displacing all their intellectual energy, aspirations, and professional ambitions onto their children, particularly their sons. It is doubtful if the current generation of Jewish women, many of whom do have their own professional identities, will hover over their children in quite the same way. In addition, parental overinvolvement may reflect the deep-seated Jewish fear, instilled by pogroms, the Holocaust, and the precariousness of the Jewish state, that the "next generation" might not survive at all.

Chaim Bermant, an English-Jewish writer, has captured the precise cadence of such parental nervousness. While working as a correspondent during the 1973 Yom Kippur War, Bermant was asked by several soldiers to telephone their parents and tell them that they were okay. When he returned from the front, he did so and kept a record of one of the conversations:

"Hullo," I began.

"Hullo? Who's that? What's that? Who are you?"

"My name is Bermant, I'm a journalist, and I've just met your son."

"My son? How is he? Where is he? Is he all right? Nothing's the matter?"

"Not a thing. He's in fine spirits, fine shape."

"And?"

"And he asked me to give you regards and to tell you not to worry."

"Not to worry? If you had a son at the front, wouldn't you worry?"

"Of course I would, and he knew you would, that's why he asked me to tell you he's fine."

"He asked you to tell me?"
"Yes."
"You mean he's not fine but he wants me to think he is?"
"No, he is fine. I saw him myself."
"Fine?"
"Perfectly."
"Then why didn't he phone me himself?"
"Because he's in the middle of the desert."
"My neighbor's son is in the middle of the desert, and he phoned."
"Maybe he was near a telephone."
"If my neighbor's son could get to a telephone, why couldn't he? I've been going crazy with worry."[2]

Other jokes focus on the hopes and fears that haunt Jewish parents. Perhaps their most prevalent desire is for *nakhas* from children (*nakhas fun kinder* is a common expression in Yiddish). *Nakhas,* meaning pleasure or contentment, is both a Hebrew and Yiddish word. Over time, however, it has come to connote the particular pride parents derived from their children's accomplishments.

What is it, according to Jewish humor, that brings parents the most *nakhas*? In the case of sons, it is professional attainments. As a "personal" in a Jewish newspaper announced:

"Mr. and Mrs. Marvin Rosenbloom are pleased to announce the birth of their son, Dr. Jonathan Rosenbloom."

Jewish parents' obsession with their sons becoming doctors is so much a part of contemporary folklore ("my son the doctor") that in the early 1960s, when Catholic leaders at the Vatican II conclave drafted a proposal to exonerate Jews from the charge of deicide, comedian Lenny Bruce stood up in a nightclub and publicly confessed:

"All right. I'll clear the air once and for all, and confess. Yes, we did it. I did it, my family. I found a note in my basement. It said:
'We killed him.
Signed,
Morty.'

"And a lot of people say to me, 'Why did you kill Christ?' . . . We killed him because he didn't want to become a doctor, that's why we killed him.'"[3]

While Bruce's wisecrack reveals nothing about the deicide charge, it says a great deal about the aspirations of contemporary Jewish parents. Tell the same joke, but attribute it to another ethnic group, and it falls flat. Imagine if Lenny Bruce had said, "We found a note left by the Roman procurator, Pontius Pilate. It says, 'We killed him because he didn't want to become a doctor, that's why we killed him.'" No one would laugh.

What about *nakhas* from daughters? With women's increasing liberation and their advancement in the American workplace, a daughter's professional attainments might soon form the basis for parental *nakhas* as well. Then again, maybe not. Although it is unfair, *nakhas* from a daughter has long been primarily based on the answers to three questions: Is she married? Does she have children? What does her husband do?

Two Jewish women who haven't seen each other in twenty years run into each other on the street.
"How's your daughter Deborah?" the first woman asks, "the one who married that lawyer?"
"They were divorced," the second woman answers.
"Oh, I'm so sorry."
"But she got married to a surgeon."
"Mazal Tov [Congratulations]."
"They were also divorced."
At this point the first woman decides to keep her mouth shut.
"But now everything is all right," her friend goes on. "She's married to a very successful architect."
The first woman shakes her head from side to side.
"Mmmm, mmmm. So much nakhas *from one daughter."*

While American-Jewish jokes generally assume that parents worry only about their daughters getting married—one rarely hears a joke about an unmarried son—in Orthodox Jewish circles, equal emphasis is placed on the marrying-off of sons. The first of the Torah's 613 laws is the command to "be fruitful and multiply" (Genesis 1:28). According to Jewish law, this obligation applies solely to men, since women cannot be forced to undergo the pain and danger of childbirth. The Talmud regards an unmarried man as one who diminishes God's presence in the world (since every baby born is another creature in God's image).

In the Orthodox world, unmarried men edging into their thirties incur increasing community disapproval and pressure. One rabbi I know postponed marriage until he was thirty-one, and then succumbed only after a very long courtship. At the wedding reception, he told the following story:

In the early years of the State of Israel, the entire Jewish community of Yemen was airlifted there. Many of the arriving immigrants claimed tremendous old ages; some of them said they were a hundred and forty, a hundred and fifty, even a hundred and sixty years old. It seemed hard to believe, and it was impossible to substantiate their claims, for they had brought no accurate birth records with them.

One day, a newly resettled Yemenite Jew appeared in the Tel Aviv office of an insurance broker saying he wanted to buy a life insurance policy. The broker looked at the man, saw he was no youngster, and asked him: "How old are you?"

"Seventy-two."

"Seventy-two? That's too old. We can't sell you a life insurance policy."

"That's not fair," the man answered. "Last week you sold my father a policy."

"Your father? How old is he?"

"Ninety-five."

"Impossible."

"Go check your records."

The agent checked his records and found to his amazement that the preceding week the man's ninety-five-year-old father had applied for a policy, that a physician had found him to be in perfect health, and that he had been issued a policy. The agent came back.

"You're right. We sold your father a policy, we'll sell you one. But you have to come in on Tuesday for a medical checkup."

"I can't come in on Tuesday."
"Why not?"
"My grandfather is getting married."
"Your grandfather is getting married? How old is he?"
"A hundred and seventeen."
"A hundred and seventeen? Why is he getting married?"
"His parents keep pestering him."

Once the children are married, in-laws come in for their fair share of cracks, but overconcern with their children-in-law's welfare is hardly the crime of which they're accused:

In a small nineteenth-century Russian shtetl, two families negotiate with a prominent yeshiva to provide two students as husbands for their daughters. The two young men set out for the town. En route, their wagon is attacked by Cossacks, and one of the men is killed. When the survivor finally arrives in the town, a fight breaks out between the mothers of the two unmarried girls: Each claims that the young man is the intended groom for her daughter. The man himself can shed no light on the matter, and the case is brought before the local rabbi.

"Cut the boy in half," the rabbi finally rules, "and let each girl be given half of his body."

"Oh, no!" the first mother says. "Don't kill him. My daughter will give up her claim."

"Go ahead and cut," the other mother says.

The rabbi stands up and points to the second woman. "That is the mother-in-law."

In-law jokes usually are as hostile and cruel as JAP jokes, and represent the kind of tasteless humor generally omitted from this book. But the foregoing story can be regarded as an exception, both because of its inherent absurdity and, more significantly, because of its witty reworking of the biblical tale about the wise King Solomon (I Kings 3:16–28): Two prostitutes come before Solomon for his judgment on a particularly difficult case. The first prostitute tells the king that a few days earlier they had each given birth to boys. The preceding night, however, the other woman's son had died and she had switched the dead baby with hers. When she got up to nurse her child, she immediately recognized that the dead baby in her arms was not her child. The second woman insists that the story is a fabrication and that no switch occurred.

Solomon asks that a sword be brought to him. "Cut the live child in two," he rules, "and give half to one, and half to the other."

One of the women begs him not to cut the baby. "Give her the live child, only don't kill him."

"Cut it in two," the other woman says.

Whereupon Solomon recognizes the merciful woman as the real mother, just as the rabbi in Jewish humor recognizes the unmerciful woman as the real mother-in-law.

From the Parents' Perspective

"Insanity is hereditary," claimed the late Jewish comedian Sam Levenson. "You can get it from your children."

Almost all the jokes related so far—mocking Jewish parents' overambitiousness, intrusiveness, and nervousness—have reflected the children's sensibility. Similarly, Sophie Portnoy, the overbearing mother of Philip Roth's *Portnoy's Complaint,* represents one man's revenge on all such "Jewish mothers." There is no comparably devastating work by a Jewish mother about Jewish sons, probably because parental love for children is usually more uncomplicated and protectve than children's love for parents. Yet the ancient Hebrew expression *tza'ar gidul banim,* "the pain of raising children," expresses a long-standing recognition that children do not provide unmitigated joy.

Two women, good friends, leave their teenagers at home for a few days and check into a fancy resort. Just before dinner, one of the women invites the other to join her in the bar for a martini.

"I never drink," the woman answers.

"Why not?"

"In front of the children, I don't think it's right to drink. And when I'm away from the children, who needs to?"

Of course, some parents sacrifice too much for their children:

A hundred-and-one-year-old man and his ninety-nine-year-old wife come before a judge. They want a divorce.
"How long have you been married?" the judge asks.
"Seventy-nine years."
"And how long have you been unhappy?"
"Almost the whole time."
"So why do you want a divorce now?"
"We were waiting for the children to die."

A mother goes into her son's room. "You've got to get up for school, Bernie."
Bernie pulls the blanket over his head. "I don't wanna go to school."
"You have to go," the mother says.
"I don't wanna. The teachers don't like me, and all the kids make fun of me."
The mother pulls the blanket down. "Bernie, you don't have any choice. You have to go to school."
"Yeah," Bernie says. "Give me one good reason!"
"You're fifty-two years old and you're the principal."

The preceding joke brings to mind a Yiddish proverb, *Kleine kinder, kleine tzoros; grosse kinder, grosse tzoros,* "Small children, small problems; big children, big problems."

A Final Joke

How do we know Jesus was Jewish?

Four reasons:

1. *He was thirty, unmarried, and still living with his mother.*
2. *He went into his father's business.*
3. *He thought his mother was a virgin.*
4. *And his mother thought he was God.*

2

"Two Men Come Down a Chimney"
Jewish Intelligence and the Playful Logic
of the Jewish Mind

▶

Jewish Brains, Jewish Braininess

In the early 1900s, an old Jew is traveling alone in his compartment on the Trans-Siberian Railroad. The train stops and an officer in the czar's army gets on. He and the Jew travel for a while in silence. Suddenly the officer grabs the Jew by the lapels and demands: "Tell me, why are you Jews so much brighter than everyone else?"

The Jew is silent a moment, then responds: "It's because of the herring we eat."

The officer quiets down and the trip resumes. Soon the Jew takes out a piece of herring and starts to eat it. The officer asks him: "How many more pieces of herring do you have?"

"A dozen."

"How much do you want for them?"

"Twenty rubles," a big sum of money.

The officer takes out the money and gives it to the Jew. The old man gives him the herring, and the officer takes a bite. Suddenly he stops. "This is ridiculous," he says. "In Moscow I could have bought all this herring for a few kopecks."

"You see," says the Jew, "it's working already."

Many Jews believe that Jews have a proportionately higher percentage of bright people than do other groups. In Eastern Europe, Jews were wont to contrast a presumably intelligent *yiddishe kop* (Jewish head) with a supposedly duller *goyishe kop* (gentile head). In the United States, many nonreligious, even unaffiliated, Jews oppose their children marrying gentiles, often because they feel that at some level a non-Jewish spouse will be less intelligent and substantial than a Jewish one.

The success of Ernest van den Haag's *The Jewish Mystique* was largely due to the book's opening chapter, in which the author, a non-Jew, presents a genetic argument for Jewish intellectual superiority. Van den Haag notes that in medieval Europe, people almost always remained in the class into which they were born. Among Christians, the only route a poor but intelligent male could take to break out of poverty was to become a priest. Many of the most intelligent but poor Christian men did exactly that, and so became celibate. This had a very detrimental effect on Christian society: "... the most intelligent portion of the population did not have offspring; their genes were siphoned off, generation after generation, into the church, and not returned to the world's, or even the church's, genetic supply."[1]

In contrast, a poor Jewish boy who excelled as a yeshiva student was likely to be married off to the daughter of a successful businessman. These arranged marriages resulted in many of the most intelligent Jews becoming affluent and thus financially capable of raising and educating a large number of children.

Some Jews, however, find such claims of intellectual superiority to be self-centered and silly. Woody Allen, in one of his parodies of Martin Buber's *Tales of the Hasidim,* tells us:

Rabbi Zwi Chaim Yisroel, an Orthodox scholar of the Torah and a man who developed whining to an art unheard of in the West, was unanimously hailed as the wisest man of the Renaissance by his fellow Hebrews, who totaled a sixteenth of one percent of the population.[2]

Woody Allen's sarcasm aside, there is some basis for the claim that Jews have a higher percentage of intellectual giants than do gentiles. For example, given that Jews comprise less than one third of 1 percent of the world's population, a Jew should win a Nobel Prize about once every thirty years. Instead, Jews have won so many Nobels that if, in any given year, no Jews win, many of them suspect antisemitism. In the United States, where Jews make up a little over 2 percent of the population, they have received 27 percent of the Prizes awarded American scientists.[3]

American Jews are twice as likely as non-Jews to attend college. They also are greatly overrepresented in the professions, particularly in medicine and law. So great is Jewish overrepresentation in many of the arts that violinist Isaac Stern described the American-Russian cultural exchange as follows: "They send us their Jews from Odessa and we send them *our* Jews from Odessa." These achievements are attributable in part to innate ability, but in part also to the fierce emphasis that traditional Jewish culture places on intellectual accomplishments, which has caused many Jews to become overachievers.

An old American-Jewish riddle asks:

Which Jew becomes an accountant?
A Jewish boy who stutters and who can't stand the sight of
blood.

Such a joke is an odd combination of self-denigration and pride; it mocks Jewish arrogance, while taking for granted Jewish intelligence. Thus, a recent contribution to the abortion debate:

According to the Catholics, a fetus becomes a full human being
at the moment of conception. According to the Jews, a fetus re-
mains a fetus until it graduates from medical school.

The Jews' conceit about their intelligence is shared by many non-Jews.[4] A common genre of ethnic and religious humor is a story featuring a minister, a priest, and a rabbi. In the Orthodox Jewish neighborhood where I was raised, I heard many such jokes—and invariably the rabbi was given the punch line. I always assumed that in the Catholic versions, the priest came out on top, and in the Protestant ones, the minister. So I was quite surprised when I interviewed Father Andrew Greeley and learned that in the jokes he had heard from other Catholics, the rabbi also received the punch line.

Oddly, even antisemites seem to believe in Jews' superior intelligence. This belief is one characteristic that distinguishes Jew-hatred from other prejudices. Prejudiced people usually dismiss the objects of their hatred as mentally inferior. But while antisemites routinely tell jokes depicting Jews as cheap or dishonest, they don't tell ones about stupid Jews.

From the antisemites' perspective, however, Jewish intelligence is hardly a virtue; Jews, they claim, use their brains for malevolent purposes. In 1610, the University of Vienna's medical faculty officially proclaimed that Jewish law requires Jewish doctors to kill one out of every ten of their Christian patients.[5] (Imagine waiting in a Jewish doctor's office, with nine people in front of you.) A half-century earlier, Martin Luther had declared: "If they [the Jews] could kill us all, they would gladly do so, aye, and often do it, especially those who profess to be physicians. They know all that is known about medicine in Germany; they can give poison to a man of which he will die in an hour, or in ten or twenty years."[6] As recently as 1953, Joseph Stalin revived Luther's accusation by charging a group of physicians, almost all of whom were Jews, with plotting to murder him and the rest of the Soviet leadership. Only Stalin's death, less than a week before the doctors' trial was to begin, saved them from execution and the rest of Russia's Jews from exile to Siberia.[7]

In the joke about herring and Jewish intelligence, the czarist officer, a presumed antisemite by virtue of his position in

44

the highly antisemitic Russian Army, believes that Jews are more intelligent. Jews laugh because they probably agree, and, more important, because brains defeat brawn; an old, presumably frail Jew outwits a soldier.

Still, why do we laugh so unselfconsciously? Should it not bother us that we are laughing at a foolish man defrauded of twenty rubles by a crafty Jew? Why do we feel no sympathy for the officer? Perhaps for two reasons: First, anyone so gullible as to believe that intelligence can be acquired by eating a certain food deserves whatever happens to him. Second, and more important, we know that this is just a joke, funny because of the point at which it ends. Only in jokes do such tricks succeed. Had a Jew really played such a trick on an army officer, he would have been beaten up, the money taken back, and the Jew lucky not to wind up in prison.

In Europe, Jews often felt they had to be "smarter-than-thou" because braininess was crucial in life-or-death situations:

A medieval Jewish astrologer prophesied to a king that his favorite mistress would soon die. Sure enough, the woman died a short time later. The king was outraged at the astrologer, certain that his prophecy had brought about the woman's death. He summoned the astrologer and commanded him: "Prophesy to me when you will die!"

The astrologer realized that the king was planning to kill him immediately, no matter what answer he gave. "I do not know when I will die," he answered finally. "I only know that whenever I die, the king will die three days later."

Beyond the need to be clever when confronting antisemitism, Jewish intellectual achievements are linked to a traditional love of learning. So a Jewish joke ridiculing education is a rarity:

A Jew comes from Europe to the Lower East Side and applies for the job of shammes *at the Rivington Street Synagogue. The synagogue's leaders are ready to hire him when they find out that he is illiterate. They decide it would not be appropriate for the synagogue to hire such a man.*

The Jew leaves, and starts peddling merchandise door to door. He does well, and soon purchases a horse and wagon. He continues to do well, and opens a store. Then another. Finally, he is ready to open five more stores, but he needs a bank loan.

He meets with the bank president, and asks for a fifty-thousand-dollar loan. The president grants it, and gives him the contract to sign. The man puts down an X.

The president is shocked. "Are you illiterate?"

The man nods.

"And even so," the president says, "you were able to build up such a big business. Imagine what you would have accomplished had you been able to read and write."

"Yes," the man says. "I would be the shammes *of the Rivington Street Synagogue."*

For Jews study has always been a holy act. In Hebrew, the word for parent, *horeh,* comes from the same root as the word for teacher, *moreh.* One of the Torah's 613 commandments decrees, "And you shall teach it [the Torah] to your children" (Deuteronomy 6:7). Nearly two thousand years ago, the Talmud mandated the establishment of schools in every city, and limited classroom size to no more than twenty-five students per teacher.

In Eastern Europe, both parents would ceremoniously lead a boy to the classroom on his first day in school, and give him sweets when he learned the *aleph-beis* (ABC's). Isaac Bashevis Singer, the Nobel Prize-winning novelist who grew up in Poland, claimed that the first day of school was more joyously celebrated than the Bar Mitzvah. The page of Torah text in front of the child, Singer recalled, was sprinkled with raisins and candy to associate learning with sweetness.

The Jewish love affair with education has continued in America. A *New York Times* article on the training of real estate brokers notes the guidelines given for selling to different groups: "If they're rich, tell them about the country club, and the high quality of people they'll meet there. If they're a young couple buying their first home, emphasize the low property taxes. If they're Jews, tell them how good the school system is."

At first reading, the joke about the illiterate *shammes*-turned-businessman seems a startling antithesis to the Jewish veneration of education. But while mocking the value of schooling, it simultaneously reinforces the belief in Jewish braininess. While other people might need to go to school to become successful, this Jew is so bright that even his illiteracy proves no obstacle to his entrepreneurial achievements.

The Talmud

A young man in his mid-twenties knocks on the door of the noted scholar Rabbi Shwartz.

"My name is Sean Goldstein," he says. "I've come to you because I wish to study Talmud."

"Do you know Aramaic?" the rabbi asks.

"No."

"Hebrew?"

"No."

"Have you studied Torah?"

"No, Rabbi. But don't worry. I graduated Berkeley summa cum laude in philosophy, and just finished my doctoral dissertation at Harvard on Socratic logic. So now, I would just like to round out my education with a little study of the Talmud."

"I seriously doubt," the rabbi says, "that you are ready to study Talmud. It is the deepest book of our people. If you wish, however, I am willing to examine you in logic, and if you pass the test I will teach you Talmud."

The young man agrees.

Rabbi Shwartz holds up two fingers. "Two men come down a chimney. One comes out with a clean face, the other comes out with a dirty face. Which one washes his face?"

The young man stares at the rabbi. "Is that the test in logic?"

The rabbi nods.

"The one with the dirty face washes his face," he answers wearily.

"Wrong. The one with the clean face washes his face. Examine the simple logic. The one with the dirty face looks at the one with the clean face and thinks his face is clean.

The one with the clean face looks at the one with the dirty face and thinks his face is dirty. So the one with the clean face washes his face."

"Very clever," Goldstein says. "Give me another test."

The rabbi again holds up two fingers. "Two men come down a chimney. One comes out with a clean face, the other comes out with a dirty face. Which one washes his face?"

"We've already established that. The one with the clean face washes his face."

"Wrong. Each one washes his face. Examine the simple logic. The one with the dirty face looks at the one with the clean face and thinks his face is clean. The one with the clean face looks at the one with the dirty face and thinks his face is dirty. So the one with the clean face washes his face. When the one with the dirty face sees the one with the clean face wash his face, he also washes his face. So each one washes his face."

"I didn't think of that," says Goldstein. "It's shocking to me that I could make an error in logic. Test me again."

The rabbi holds up two fingers. "Two men come down a chimney. One comes out with a clean face, the other comes out with a dirty face. Which one washes his face?"

"Each one washes his face."

"Wrong. Neither one washes his face. Examine the simple logic. The one with the dirty face looks at the one with the clean face and thinks his face is clean. The one with the clean face looks at the one with the dirty face and thinks his face is dirty. But when the one with the clean face sees that the one with the dirty face doesn't wash his face, he also doesn't wash his face. So neither one washes his face."

Goldstein is desperate. "I am qualified to study Talmud. Please give me one more test."

He groans, though, when the rabbi lifts two fingers. "Two men come down a chimney. One comes out with a clean face, the other comes out with a dirty face. Which one washes his face?"

"Neither one washes his face."

"Wrong. Do you now see, Sean, why Socratic logic is an insufficient basis for studying Talmud? Tell me, how is it possible for two men to come down the same chimney, and for one to come out with a clean face and the other with a dirty face? Don't you see? The whole question is narishkeit, *foolishness, and if you spend your life trying to answer foolish questions, all your answers will also be foolish."*[8]

In traditional Jewish culture, braininess primarily manifests itself in one field of study, the Talmud. And although the non-Jewish world has often regarded the Talmud as a perverse form of Jewish thinking (the term in English "talmudic mind" is used to describe nit-picking logic), to Orthodox Jews it has always represented the pinnacle of wisdom. Sean Goldstein (perhaps named after his grandfather Shmuel; one looks in vain for an Irish Shmuel named for his grandfather Sean), holder of a Ph.D. in philosophy, believes he is being broad-minded in rounding out his education with a little Talmud study. To Rabbi Shwartz, Socratic logic, a Berkeley *summa cum laude,* and a Harvard Ph.D. carry no great intellectual weight. How can a young man who doesn't know Hebrew, and who's never studied Torah, have the chutzpah to think that he is ready to study Talmud, the most profound work ever produced?

But the rabbi's intellectual assault on Sean Goldstein contains more than annoyance at the young man's arrogance. Religious Jews have long harbored skepticism about just the kind of academic thinking in which Sean has been trained. Great mental efforts seem to be exerted by philosophers on pointless pursuits (secular Jews who study philosophy are prone to think the same thing about Jews who study Talmud). Immanuel Kant, one of philosophy's giants, was unwilling to state categorically that anyone besides himself existed—perhaps all other people were figments of his imagination. For a century after Kant, philosophers wore themselves out trying to answer this challenge. Hence Rabbi Shwartz's warning: "If you spend your life trying to answer foolish questions, all your answers will also be foolish."

The Talmud itself opposes abstract thinking that is unrelated to reality. Consider this talmudic excerpt, with its Woody Allenesque punch line:

> *If a fledgling bird is found within fifty cubits [about seventy-five feet] ... [of a man's property], it belongs to the owner of the property. If it is found outside the limits of fifty cubits, it belongs to the person who finds it.*
>
> *Rabbi Jeremiah asked the question: "If one foot of the fledg-*

ling bird is within the limit of fifty cubits, and one foot is outside it, what is the law?"

It was for this question that Rabbi Jeremiah was thrown out of the house of study (Bava Bathra 23b).[9]

Yet, the rabbis of the Talmud were as adept as philosophers at making their legal discussions quite abstract, while fervently denying that their speculations were impractical. The cases they analyzed, even the most theoretical ones, were for them always potential realities.

Consider the biblical injunction that Jews should eat only unleavened products during Passover, and remove all leavened products from their homes before the holiday. Consequently, every room in a house where a person might have consumed bread or other leavened products, such as cake, has to be scrupulously cleaned and all the crumbs removed. But what if a room was thoroughly cleaned and then bread was brought into it? Must the entire cleaning procedure be repeated? This exact issue is addressed in the following talmudic discussion:

Rava [a fourth-century rabbi living in Babylonia] asked: "Suppose a mouse entered a room which had already been searched, with a piece of bread in its mouth, and a mouse then came out of the room with a piece of bread in its mouth. Can one assume that the mouse [and bread] that came out are the same mouse and bread that went in [in which case, no further search is necessary]? Or is it perhaps a different mouse?"

Rava then went on to ask: "Suppose that the answer to my first question is that there is no need to assume a different mouse: What if a white mouse went in with bread in its mouth and a black mouse came out with bread in its mouth? Must one assume that it is a different piece of bread, or can one suppose that it is the same piece of bread which the first mouse threw away and the second mouse picked up?"

Perhaps you will say, "Mice do not take food from each other." In that case, what if a mouse went in with a piece of bread in its mouth and a weasel came out with a piece of bread in its mouth? Can one assume that the weasel took away the bread from the mouse, or could it be another piece of bread, since a weasel would have the mouse itself in its mouth? Suppose

50

*then that the weasel had the mouse and the bread in its mouth?
But surely if it were the same piece of bread, the weasel would
have the mouse in its mouth and the bread would still be in the
mouse's mouth? But perhaps the mouse dropped the bread in its
fear and the weasel picked up the mouse and the bread sepa-
rately?*
The problem was left unsolved (Pesachim *10b).*[10]

It should be apparent how much the rabbis delighted in
subtle, if often theoretical, arguments. Inevitably, the Talmud's
insistence on examining every possible nuance and conse-
quence of an act shaped the minds of those who spent many
years studying it. Hence arose the popular image among Jews
of a talmudic scholar, a person who, on the basis of pure logic
and a minimum of evidence, reaches penetrating and startling
conclusions.

The following story is so characteristically Jewish that one
finds some form of it in virtually every collection of Jewish humor (I have followed closely the version told in Simon Pollack's
Jewish Wit):

*Mr. Goldstein is returning by train from New York City to Glens
Falls, a small town in upstate New York. Seated next to him on
the train is a young man he doesn't know. As the ride is long,
Goldstein starts a conversation with the young man. His name
is Alan Levine, and he is also heading for Glens Falls.*
"Are you going there on business?" Goldstein asks.
"No. It's a social visit."
"Do you have relatives there?"
"No."
"Are you married?"
"No, I'm not."
*Goldstein thinks to himself: "He's going to Glens Falls, he's
not married, it's not business, and he has no relatives there. So
why is he going? Obviously to meet a girl or, more likely, her
family. Perhaps to confirm their engagement? But with whom?
There are only three Jewish families apart from mine in Glens
Falls, the Resnicks, the Feldsteins, and the Cohens.*
*"It couldn't be the Resnicks. Resnick only has sons. The
Feldsteins have two girls, but one is married and the other is
studying in Europe for the year. It must be the Cohens. They have*

*three daughters: Marsha, Sheila, and Rachel. Marsha is already
married. Sheila is too plump and unattractive for this handsome
young man. So it must be Rachel. Yes, Rachel! A wonderful girl."*

*With this, Goldstein breaks the silence and smiles at the
stranger. "Well, congratulations on your forthcoming marriage
to Rachel Cohen."*

*"B . . . b . . . but," the young man stutters; "we haven't told
anybody. How did you know?"*

"Why, it's obvious," answers Goldstein.

While the joke describes a reasoning process that seems
exaggeratedly subtle, the rabbis of the Talmud probably
wouldn't have understood that the story was meant to be funny.
After all, some talmudic passages could convince one that Sher-
lock Holmes either was a Jew, or at least that he had spent
several years in a yeshiva. One can easily imagine the young
Holmes poring over the following account from the Talmud:

*It once happened that two Jews were taken captive on Mount
Carmel. As their captor walked behind them, one of the captives
said to the other, "The camel which has preceded us on this road
is blind in one eye and is carrying two pouches, one filled with
wine and the other containing oil. As for the men leading the
camel, one of them is a Jew, while the other is a heathen."*

*Their captor, overhearing this, said to them: ". . . How do
you know this?"*

*And he was told: "From the grass, which is close-cropped on
only one side of the road; from the side on which the camel is
able to see, he ate, while the other side has been left untouched.
It is also clear that the camel is carrying two saddlebags, one
filled with wine and the other with oil; for drops of wine are
absorbed [into the ground, accounting for the dampness of the
earth], while drops of oil remain on the surface of the road and
can be seen. It is also certain that one of the men leading the
camel is a Jew and the other is not; for a Jew leaves the road
to perform his natural functions [the evidence of which can be
seen on the side of the road], while others do not."*

*Their captor continued to follow them, and when they over-
took the camel ahead of them, he found that it was indeed as
they had said. He kissed them on their heads, brought them to
his home, prepared a meal for them and waited upon them. . . .*

He then set them free, and they returned in peace to their homes" (Sanhedrin *104a).*[11]

The only thing missing in this story is for the slaves to shrug their shoulders and say, "It was obvious."

The Kal Va-Khomer, a Talmudic Principle of Logic

The Talmud's best known logical argument is the *kal va-khomer,* which, in the classic Soncino Press translation, is rendered as the Latin *a fortiori.* Since few people today know Latin, a more useful translation would be "how much more so," as for example, "If a country's legal code sentences people to death for stealing, *kal va-khomer* will do so for premeditated murder."

The Talmud credits Moses with being the originator of the *kal va-khomer.* In his last oration to the Hebrews, he employs this form of reasoning to express concern over their disloyalty: "If you have been rebellious against God while I was yet alive with you, how much more so will you be after my death?" (Deuteronomy 31:27). At the beginning of his career, Moses had even turned the *kal va-khomer* against God's command that he demand the Jews' freedom from Pharaoh: "And if the children of Israel don't listen to me, how is Pharaoh going to listen?" (Exodus 6:12).

Among knowledgeable Eastern European Jews, the *kal va-khomer* became a favorite target of Jewish wit. Irving Kristol, the intellectual godfather of neoconservative thought as well as an authority on Jewish humor, cites a demented Talmud scholar's *kal va-khomer:*

If I have the right to take money out of my pocket, from which the other man has no right to take money, then is not my right all the greater to take money from his pocket, from which even he has the right to take money?[12]

The rabbis of the Talmud understood that theoretical arguments could be marshaled to make any legal system seem absurd. The first-century rabbi Yossi ben Taddai of Tiberias loved to employ the *kal va-khomer* to reach ludicrous deductions. He once challenged Rabbi Gamliel:

> *I am forbidden to marry my daughter, but my daughter's mother is permitted to me. All the more so, then, I should be forbidden to marry the daughter of someone who is forbidden to me. [Since] I am forbidden to marry somebody else's wife, I should be forbidden to marry the daughter of somebody else's wife. Therefore, all marriages should be forbidden [except, as Hyam Maccoby has noted, for marriages to the daughters of unmarried mothers, widows, or divorcees].[13]*

Rabbi Gamliel, the intellectual leader of Rabbi Yossi's generation, had many virtues, but a sense of humor apparently was not one of them. Fearing that Rabbi Yossi's jokes would cause rabbinical modes of argument to be dismissed as ridiculous, he excommunicated him.

Echoes of the *kal va-khomer* can be heard even in stories about purely secular matters. Felix Mendelsohn, in *The Jew Laughs*, tells this classic Eastern European story:

> *Two yeshiva students, Sender and Mendel, were discussing the rumors of war which threatened to engulf all Europe in July, 1914. Mendel was terribly pessimistic about the future, but Sender tried to console him.*
>
> *"If I were you, I would not worry yet," said Sender. "This entire affair may blow over, but even if there should be a war, you still have two possibilities: You may be sent to fight at the front or you may not be sent to fight at the front. If you are not sent to the front you have nothing to worry about, but even if you should be sent to the front, there are still two possibilities: You will either be wounded or you will not be wounded. If you are not wounded you have nothing to worry about, but even if you are wounded you still have two possibilities: You may be wounded slightly or you may be wounded seriously. If you are wounded slightly you have nothing to worry about, but if you are wounded seriously you still have two possibilities: You may*

*either die from your wound or you may not die. If you do not
die you have nothing to worry about, but even if you do die
you still have two possibilities: You may either go to the good
place or to the bad place. If you go to the good place you have
nothing to worry about, but even if you do go to the bad place,
you still have one possibility: War may not be declared, so you
still have nothing to worry about.*"[14]

My favorite "talmudic" story actually has nothing to do with the
Talmud. When I was a student at Yeshiva University, there was
a rabbinic scholar—I will refer to him as Rabbi Levy—who became blind in his later years. Nonetheless, because he knew so
much of the Talmud and its commentaries by heart, he was able
to continue giving his daily Talmud *shiur* (class). Unfortunately,
Rabbi Levy knew the name of only one student, Goldstein, and
every day he called on him to read and explain the talmudic
portion being studied. This was driving Goldstein crazy, so one
morning, when Rabbi Levy said, "Nu, Goldstein, read the Talmud," the student spoke up in a falsetto voice, "Goldstein is
not here today." Rabbi Levy paused a moment, then responded,
"Goldstein's not here? Then you read the Talmud."

Reason Gone Mad: The Humor of the Absurd

*The time is at hand when the wearing of a prayer shawl and a
skullcap will not bar a man from the White House—unless, of
course, the man is Jewish. —Jules Farber, in Wallace Markfield,*
You Could Live If They Let You

Absurdist humor, like that inspired by the Talmud, is
rooted in paradox and irony. Thus, because Judaism believes
that a perfect God created this world, it must make sense. Yet
Jewish history, filled with antisemitic violence and other injus-
tices, suggests that much that occurs in this world makes no
sense at all. Hence, Wallace Markfield's irreverent rumination
on American pluralism. As much as Jewish values influence the
general culture—Christianity, after all, started as a Jewish

sect—the culture is still unwilling to accept the Jews.

The most notable exemplar of this lack of acceptance was Martin Luther, whose revolt against the Catholic Church in the sixteenth century was fueled largely by his understanding of the Hebrew Bible. Indeed, he translated the Bible into German, but, as he later noted: "I endeavored to make Moses so German that no one would suspect he was a Jew"—an unintentionally comic premonition of Wallace Markfield's quip.

More than any other genre of Jewish humor, the absurdist often falls into the category of "laughing in order not to cry."

A man comes to the head of the burial society; he needs a loan to pay for the funeral of his wife, who has just died.
   "But we gave you money to bury your wife three years ago," the head of the burial society tells him.
   "Yes, but I remarried."
   "Oh, I didn't know. Mazal Tov!"

Aside from mocking the *world's* irrationalities, absurdist humor takes on *human* irrationalities:

A Jewish woman is wheeling her grandson in a baby carriage.
   A woman stops her. "What a beautiful baby," she says.
   "Ah, this is nothing! You should see his pictures."

The grandmother is guilty of a common failing: an aversion to reality. What matters is not who we truly are, but what image we wish to project. That is why people smile in photographs even when they are sad.

Groucho Marx was particularly adept at pointing out the fatal flaw in popular, but irrational, beliefs (see his comment on antisemitism on page 109). Leo Rosten, a friend of Groucho's, recounts how the comedian once punctured the aura surrounding a well-known spiritualist:

In Hollywood, people were captivated by a man who held costly seances during which he displayed supernatural powers.
   Groucho was encouraged to go to one.
   The spiritualist went around the table summoning up long-

dead parents, relaying messages to and from the dead, making astonishing predictions, and confidently answering questions about all things.

Finally, after two hours, the spiritualist said: "My medium angel is getting tired. I have time for only one more question. You can find out anything you want."

Groucho called out: "What's the capital of North Dakota?"[15]

Three on Restaurants

There are a surprising number of jokes about Jewish restaurants, and absurdity seems to lie at the heart of them. For one thing, even Jewish foods, or at least their names, evoke laughter. As Steve Allen explains: "Words like lox, herring, chopped liver, chicken soup and matza are inherently more amusing than trout, bass, lamb stew, vegetable soup and whole wheat bread."[16] F. Scott Fitzgerald reportedly walked into delicatessens just to hear people say *knish.*

Perhaps the best-known Jewish food word is "kosher." In contemporary America, the word has acquired a positive connotation; it signifies cleanliness and purity. Many kosher products, particularly meats, are bought by non-Jews and nonreligious Jews, who are convinced that they are of higher quality. This early-twentieth-century American-Jewish joke indicates that this perception might be of more recent vintage:

Two men come into a restaurant on the Lower East Side of Manhattan. The first one asks for tea.

The second also asks for tea. "And make sure the glass is clean," he tells the waiter.

The waiter returns with two glasses of tea. "Now who asked for the clean one?" he says.

The following joke turns on the Yiddish expression *"Aha!"* so often used as the clinching line in an argument. In only three letters, it connotes: "Do you now see not only that I am right, but how foolish you have been in arguing with me all this time?"

Goldstein has been going to the same restaurant on the Lower East Side for ten years. Every day, he starts with the same thing, barley soup. One day, as soon as he comes in, the waiter brings the soup over to his table.

"I want you should taste the barley soup," Goldstein says as the waiter starts to walk away.

"What's the matter?" the waiter says. "Every day, you take the barley soup."

"I want you should taste the barley soup," Goldstein repeats.

"You don't want the barley soup?" the waiter says. "I'll bring you something else."

"I want you should taste the barley soup," Goldstein repeats.

"Okay, okay, I'll taste the barley soup," the waiter says wearily. "Where's the spoon?"

"Aha!"

In another Jewish restaurant, a man comes in and his order is taken by a Chinese waiter who speaks perfect Yiddish.

After the waiter takes his order and goes to the kitchen, the man calls over the manager.

"Where did you find a Chinese waiter who knows Yiddish?"

"Shh!" the manager says. "He thinks he's learning English."

Chelm

The oldest absurdist jokes are the ones about Chelm, which date back to the nineteenth century. The citizens of Chelm, an actual city in Poland, were for unknown reasons stigmatized as idiots. Most Chelm jokes are distasteful, depicting the townspeople as so foolish that laughing at them is like laughing at the retarded. However, the best Chelm jokes are not about stupidity, but rather about a naïveté so extraordinary that the listeners are catapulted to a new vision of reality. Los Angeles comedian Larry Wilde tells the following:

Hockman, the Hebrew teacher, and Luchinsky, the rabbi of Chelm, were sipping tea and discussing the town's economy.

"There is great injustice heaped on the poor," sighed Hockman. "The rich, who have more money than they need, can buy on credit. But the poor, who haven't two coins to knock together, have to pay cash for everything. Is that fair?"

"Of course," answered the rabbi.

"But it should be the other way around," insisted Hockman. "The rich, who have money, should pay cash, and the poor should be able to buy on credit."

"I admire your ideals," said the rabbi. "But a merchant who extends credit to the poor instead of the rich will soon become a poor man himself."

"So," retorted the Hebrew teacher. "Then he'd be able to buy on credit too!"[17]

Or consider this one:

A Hebrew teacher in Chelm declared one day:
"If I was Rothschild I would be richer than Rothschild."
"Why?"
"Because I would give Hebrew lessons on the side."

Jews from Chelm hear the same words we hear but understand them differently:

A Jew from Chelm visits Warsaw. In the main shul (synagogue), he hears the shammes ask a riddle: "Who is my father's son but not my brother?"

No one knows.

"It's me," the shammes says.

The Chelm Jew is very impressed. He returns home and, after shul, asks: "Who is my father's son but not my brother?"

No one knows. So the Chelm Jew answers, "The shammes in Warsaw."

In *Arab Political Humor,* Khalid Kishtainy presents an Egyptian equivalent of this story, but with more bite in terms of social criticism:

A poor woman was repeatedly irritated by her husband's preoccupation with politics and enthusiasm for [former Egyptian Pres-

ident Gamal Abdel] Nasser and his Socialist Union Party. "Look at you! What have you gained out of Nasser and all your talk about his party? Why don't you go and ask him? What have we gained out of him?"

The woman dared her husband and the wretched man decided to take up her challenge and go and see the leader. After listening to the story, Nasser asked him to go to the window and tell him what he saw. There were the beautiful presidential gardens, the well-kept streets around, the lofty palaces and four-star hotels of Cairo. "Now go to your wife and tell her," said Nasser, "in ten more years under the Socialist Union, the whole of Egypt will be like this."

The man was very impressed and hurried home to tell his wife. "Go to the window and tell me what you see." The wife went to the window of their hovel and started to [describe what she saw]. There was the open cesspit stinking in the heat, the children, in rags, fighting over a moldy biscuit, the rubbish heap, the rusty dumped cars, etc., etc. "Ten more years under the Socialist Union and the whole of Egypt will be like this," said her husband.[18]

Pseudointellectual Absurdities

A story in which the speaker pretends to know something, but is finally shown to be as ignorant as his listeners, might be called a "pseudointellectual absurdity." Here is one nineteenth-century example:

A Jew asks his friend: "How does the telegraph system work? I don't understand how they can transmit a message over wires."

His friend says: "Forget the wires. Imagine instead a giant dog, with his head in Kovno and his tail in Vilna. Pull the tail in Vilna, and the dog will bark in Kovno."

"I see," the friend says. "But how does wireless telegraphy work?"

"The very same way, but without the dog."[19]

Two thousand years ago, the Talmud admonished: "Teach your tongue to say, 'I don't know.'" Yet because Jewish culture places so much stress on intellectual achievement, such confessions, even in minor matters, do not come easily to Jews.*

In the above story, neither of the Jews understands how the telegraph works, but only one admits it. Folklorist Immanuel Olsvanger notes that variants of this story have circulated in the Russian and Arab worlds. Those versions, however, generally end with "Pull the tail in Vilna, and the dog will bark in Kovno"—or a similar line. According to Olsvanger: "The significance of the Jewish version, [however], lies in the super-climax that renders the original conclusion of the story a mere pseudo-climax. ... The teller enjoys teasing his audience, and when it laughs at the pseudo-climax he is at his happiest, and is able to say: 'Fools, why the laughter? The real joke is yet to come!' Then those who laughed feel like those who applaud a musical performer before he has played his piece to its end."[20]

Goldstein tells his friend Silver: "Life is like a bowl of tuna fish."
   Silver is quiet for a minute, then says: "Why is life like a bowl of tuna fish?"
   "How should I know? Am I a philosopher?"

In an alternate version, Goldstein shrugs his shoulders and says, "So it's not like a bowl of tuna fish."

*Israelis, for example, are notorious for offering directions to questioning tourists even to places with which they are unfamiliar.

3

"So How Do You Make a Hurricane?"
The Jew in Business, or Jokes That Would
Give an Antisemite *Nakhas*

▶

Jewish Business Ethics

An Italian barber, giving a man a haircut, learns that his client is a Protestant minister. When it comes time to pay, the barber says, "Reverend, of course I am not a Protestant. But I respect any man of God. I will not accept money from you." The minister is very touched, thanks the barber, goes out, and an hour later comes back and gives him a beautiful edition of the New Testament.

A few days later, a man with a clerical collar comes in for a haircut. When it comes time to pay, the barber says, "Father, I, of course, am also a Catholic. I will not take money from you." The priest is very touched, thanks the barber, goes out, and an hour later comes back with a beautiful crucifix.

A few days later a man comes in for a haircut. While talking to him, the barber learns that he is a rabbi. When it comes time to pay, the barber says, "I, of course, am not a Jew. But I respect any religious leader. I will not take money from you." The rabbi is very touched, thanks the barber, and an hour later comes back with another rabbi.

In humor about Jews, no area is more sensitive than jokes about business practices and ethics. Indeed, were it not for such jokes, there would be almost no humor offensive to Jews. Stories containing slurs assigned to other groups—mob connections to Italians, stupidity to Poles and blacks, and sexual perversities to the British, Arabs, and Greeks—would not provoke laughter if told about Jews. Yet, jokes telling of "sharp" Jewish business practices are laughed at by non-Jews and, significantly, by Jews too.

What makes these jokes funny? While there certainly is no evidence that Jews are more mendacious than gentiles, those Jews who are dishonest are more likely to commit white-collar crimes than crimes of violence. In fact, Jews are shocked when they hear that "one of ours" has been arrested for rape or murder.

Yet during their early years in America, many Jews did commit violent crimes. And for some Jews those acts became a type of business. Murder Incorporated, the Mafia-linked murder-for-hire group active during the 1930s and 1940s, was founded and run by Jewish gangsters.[1]

By the time of the second and third generation in America, however, violent crimes committed by Jews had become rare. As Jackie Mason has observed:

I never saw four black people walking down the street saying, "Watch out, there's a Jew over there!" Well, let's be honest about it. Did you ever see anybody afraid to walk into a Jewish neighborhood because he might get killed by an accountant?[2]

When it comes to white-collar crime, however, an altogether different image prevails. The Jewish community was more disheartened and embarrassed than shocked when Jewish names dominated the lists of those arrested for insider stock-trading offenses during the late 1980s. In one notorious case, a police informer bugged a Friday night Shabbat dinner at his house, where the singing of "Shalom Aleichem" (a Friday evening hymn) and the recitation of the *kiddush* blessing over wine were followed by a profitable and illegal exchanging of stock tips.

Several years earlier, *The Wall Street Journal* reported the arrest of two prominent Jewish businessmen who had defrauded people in the computer industry. In investigating their backgrounds, the *Journal* learned that, some time before, they had broken with one Orthodox synagogue and established another, claiming that the barrier *(mekhitza)* separating the men's and women's section at the first synagogue was too low. Apparently it is easier for some people to cross moral barriers than ritual ones.

Why is it that a religious civilization so amazingly successful at inculcating its adherents with a hatred of physical violence, has had less success in imbuing many of them with an aversion to financial chicanery?

The answer is probably rooted in the many centuries during which Jews were discriminated against and cheated by European and Arab governments. They were often forbidden to own land and were barred from many professions. To Jews, deceiving such governments did not seem wrong, because so many discriminatory laws and taxes were directed against the Jewish community. Even the eighteenth century's leading German Jew, Moses Mendelssohn, had to pay a special head tax (imposed on Jews and cattle) upon entering his hometown of Dessau. Similar obnoxious taxes were levied against Jews throughout Europe.

In much of the Arab world, Jews—and Christians—were subjected to a special poll tax. Upon receiving the tax from the *dhimmi* (the tolerated but "second-class" Jewish or Christian resident), the emir would often strike him on the neck, and a guard would then chase the unfortunate taxpayer away. In medieval Iraq, Jewish and Christian taxpayers sometimes had the receipt for the payment stamped on their necks, in fulfillment of Mohammed's directive that Jews and Christians should be humiliated when paying their taxes because they "follow not the religion of truth" (Koran 9:29).[3]

Small wonder that Jews living in such societies did what-

ever they could to avoid paying taxes. These practices sometimes spilled over into their business dealings. Of course, many
leading rabbis decried this behavior. In the early centuries of
the Common Era, the rabbis issued a ruling that any Jew who
defrauded the customs authorities "[it] is as if he shed
blood—and not only shed blood, but also worshiped idols,
committed acts of unchastity, and profaned the Sabbath" (*Sem-
akhot* 2:9). Many hundreds of years later, in thirteenth-century
France, Rabbi Moshe of Coucy, author of a classic legal code,
ruled that Jews must be particularly honest in their dealings
with gentiles lest a Jew cheat a non-Jew and the latter then re-
solve never to convert to Judaism.[4]

Other less refined, or overly practical, rabbis permitted a
moral double standard. It was forbidden for a Jew to steal from
a non-Jew, they ruled, but if he or she made an error in a business transaction, one was not obligated to point it out.

Where Jews are treated equally by the law, as in America,
such practices are unconscionable. Yet, some Jews, like others
of all nations, find the allure of profit stronger than that of con-
science. Some of the best jokes come out of the wiles worked
in the world of insurance:

> *Levine meets his friend Shwartz. "I heard your factory burned
> down," he says.*
> *"Sh, sh," Shwartz answers, looking around anxiously. "Next
> week."*

Here is a variation on the above:

> *Levine and Shwartz meet in Miami Beach. Levine says that his
> business burned down a year earlier and everything was de-
> stroyed. The only thing that saved him from ruination was that
> he had the business insured for half a million.*
> *Shwartz says that something similar happened to him; his
> store was flooded in a hurricane. Everything in the store was
> destroyed, but fortunately he carried insurance for a million
> dollars. In fact, he even had enough money left over to open
> up a new store.*

"Wonderful, wonderful," Levine says. "But tell me, Shwartz, how do you make a hurricane?"[5]

Goldstein, an accountant, does some financial work for the Mob. When an Argentinean robber, also working for the Mob, absconds with $250,000 stolen from a bank, the Mob sends an enforcer, along with the Spanish-speaking Goldstein, to find the man. They catch up with him in Buenos Aires.

"Ask him where the money is," the enforcer tells Goldstein.

Goldstein asks the man. The bank robber says, "I won't tell you a thing."

Goldstein translates what the Argentinean has said. The enforcer shoots the man in his right knee.

"Ask him again," the enforcer says.

Again the man says, "I won't tell. I'm never going to tell."

The enforcer shoots him in the other knee.

"Tell him," the enforcer says, "that the next shot goes right through his head."

Goldstein translates the enforcer's words.

The Argentinean says, "Tell him it's in the trunk of my car, under the spare wheel."

Goldstein turns to the enforcer. "He says he's not afraid to die!"

Or consider this story from Leo Rosten's *The Joys of Yinglish*:

One of my favorite childhood memories involves a men's clothing store in our neighborhood on Roosevelt Road in Chicago, which was owned by a pair of partners ... who, rumor had it, sent eight children through college simply by—pretending to be deaf. The ingenious haberdasher's caper is unmatched, I think, for simplicity, duplicity, and proper punishment of the greedy. Here is how it worked:

One partner would wait on a customer, extolling the excellence of the wool or the styling of this or that suit. The customer would naturally ask, "How much is it?"

"What," asked the 'salesman,' cupping his ear.

"How—much—does—it—cost?" the customer repeated more loudly.

"Hanh?"

"How much is the suit?" *the customer would shout.*

"Ah, the price! ... *I'll ask the boss."*

Whereupon the "clerk" would turn and shout toward the

back of the store: "How much is the beautiful navy-blue double-breasted suit?"

The "boss" would shout back, "Forty dollars." *The "deaf" clerk would tell the customer, "The boss says, 'Twenty dollars.'"*

Need I describe how swiftly many men, young and old, plunked down their twenty dollars and hastened out of the store, chortling?[6]

In *The Jews of Modernity,* Milton Himmelfarb, a former editor of *Commentary,* tells one of only two jokes I know that feature a "Righteous Gentile," the term Jews use to describe Christians who saved Jews during the Holocaust (see page 113 for the other joke). This joke reflects a great deal about how Jews assumed their Polish neighbors perceived them:

Jews from a Polish village have survived Hitler and have established themselves as an egg and poultry cooperative in Israel. They are grateful to their friend, the peasant elder, for helping to save them from the Nazis, and they are proud of having made themselves into productive, progressive agriculturists. . . . So they pool their money and send a ticket to the old peasant, who eventually comes from Poland to visit them. They show him their modern equipment and methods and he is impressed. Then they show him how artificial light twenty-four hours a day keeps the hens laying eggs without interruption. He shakes his head and says: "Ah, Zhidy, Zhidy! You have no honest Poles to trick anymore, so you trick chickens."[7]

In a biting witticism, the early Zionist leader Vladimir Jabotinsky fused contempt for peasant simplemindedness with a hint of Jewish chicanery: "A Russian peasant once pronounced this mathematical theory: 'Four and four make eight, with this I can agree; some say five and three also make eight—but that's a Jewish trick.'"

The Khukham *in Jewish Humor*

In Hebrew the word *khakham* means "one who is wise," and is one of the highest compliments a person can be paid. A great religious scholar is called a *talmid khakham,* which is generally translated as a "student of the wise." Sephardic Jews often apply the appellation *khakham,* rather than rabbi, to leading rabbinical scholars.

In Yiddish, however, the word *khakham* became *khukham* and lost much of its luster. It acquired the connotation of "wise guy" rather than "wise," as illustrated by these stories about seven *khukhamim:*

> "A terrible thing," says Jacob to his friend. "My daughter is to be married tomorrow and I promised a dowry of five thousand rubles. Now, half the dowry is missing."
>
> "So what?" replies the friend. "One usually pays only half of the promised dowry."
>
> "That's the half that's missing."[8]

> A khukham *calls on the rabbi of a town, and asks for help. "Everything I owned, Rabbi, was lost when my house burned down in a terrible fire. I've been left with nothing."*
>
> *"Do you have a letter from the rabbi of your town attesting to this fire?" the rabbi asks.*
>
> *"I had such a letter, but that too was lost in the fire."*

In one nineteenth-century story, a rich but greedy *khukham* receives his comeuppance:

> A poor Jew finds a wallet with five hundred rubles. At synagogue, he hears that the town's wealthiest Jew has lost his wallet and is offering a fifty-ruble reward to anyone who returns it.
>
> He quickly locates the owner and gives him the wallet. The rich man counts the money and then says: "Well, I see you've already taken your reward."
>
> "What are you talking about?" the poor man says.
>
> "This wallet had five hundred and fifty rubles in it when I lost it."
>
> "That's not true."
>
> The two men start arguing, and eventually they come before the local rabbi.
>
> After both men present their case, the wealthy man says to the rabbi, "I trust you believe me, Rabbi."
>
> "Of course," the rabbi says. The rich man smiles, and the poor Jew is devastated. Then the rabbi takes the wallet out of

the wealthy man's hands, and gives it to the man who found it.
"What are you doing?" the rich man yells angrily.
"You are, of course, an honest man," the rabbi tells him.
"And if you say your missing wallet had five hundred and fifty rubles in it, I'm sure it did. But if the man who found this wallet is a liar and a thief, he wouldn't have returned it at all. Which means that this wallet must belong to somebody else. If that man steps forward, he'll get the money. Otherwise, it stays with the man who found it."
"And what about my money?" the rich man asks.
"Well, we'll just have to wait until somebody finds a wallet with five hundred and fifty rubles in it."

Most *khukham* jokes are about money, but there are exceptions. Indeed, the following *khukham* was not money-wise at all, although he was quick-witted:

A khukham left his small shtetl and went on a business trip to Kiev. In two weeks, he earned over a hundred rubles, a huge sum. The man was so excited, he telegraphed the news of his success to his wife. Then, the night before he was to return home, he lost everything he had made in a card game. He couldn't imagine how he was going to face his wife.
When he arrived home, he walked in with one hand cupped over his nose.
"What's the matter?" his wife screamed when she saw him.
"It's terrible what happened," he said. "Just outside of Kiev, a gang of bandits attacked our wagon. They made everyone step outside, and one of them said, 'If you don't turn over all your money to us, we'll cut off your nose.'"
"Oh my God," the wife says. "What's the matter with you? You should have given them all the money."
The husband removes his hand from his face.
"You're right," he says, smiling. "That's exactly what I did."

In a parallel story, a *khukham*'s quick-wittedness saves him from the wrath of a powerful gentile:

A small Jewish man is sitting on a boat deck next to a huge, sleeping Texan. The Jew gets seasick and ends up vomiting all over the Texan.

*The Texan starts to stir. He opens his eyes and, to his horror,
sees himself covered with vomit.*
"You feel better now?" the little Jew asks.

Despite the *khukham*'s negative image in Jewish humor,
Jewish folklore provides a story about a gentle *khukham:*

*The same man had served for many years as the wagon driver
for the eighteenth-century rabbi Yehezkel Landau of Prague. He
accompanied Rabbi Landau on his lecture tours. Very often, the
rabbi gave the same learned discourse, and after several years,
the driver learned it by heart.*

*Once, shortly before the two men entered a city, the driver
said to the rabbi: "In every town we go, I see the great respect
people show you. I'd like to know what it feels like to be given
such honor. I know the speech you're intending to give by heart.
Just this once, when we enter the town, could you be driving the
wagon, and let me be dressed as the rabbi and give the speech?"*

The rabbi, a compassionate man, agreed.

*They drove into the town, and everything proceeded ac-
cording to plan. The driver delivered the discourse perfectly,
while the rabbi, dressed as a wagon driver, sat in back of the
synagogue and listened.*

*When the talk was concluded, people started asking the
speaker questions. Most were repetitions of questions he had
heard for years and, remembering the responses the rabbi had
given, he easily answered them. But then a very difficult question
was raised, one that went well beyond the driver's expertise.*

*For a few seconds, he stood quietly at the lectern. "You
think that question is deep?" he finally asked. "Why it's so simple,
even my wagon driver can answer it. And just to prove to you
that I'm right, I'm going to ask him to come forward."*

This *khukham* aside, most *khukham* were tricksters, anx-
ious to get something for nothing:

*A khukham, we'll call him Goldstein, goes into a restaurant and
orders potato latkes. When they come, he complains that they
don't look good and changes his order to blintzes. After he eats
the blintzes, he stands up and starts to leave the restaurant.*

"Wait a second," the manager shouts after him.

"You haven't paid for your blintzes."

71

"What are you talking about?" Goldstein says.

"Those blintzes were only an exchange. I gave you the potato latkes for them."

"Yes, but you didn't pay for the potato latkes either."

"Why should I pay for them? I didn't eat them!"

Materialism

An elderly Jewish woman, hovering near death, calls in a rabbi.

"I have two requests before I die," she says. "First, I want to be cremated."

"But that's absolutely forbidden," the rabbi answers. "Jewish law considers cremation the grossest disrespect to a dead body."

"I don't care," the woman says, "I want to be cremated."

The argument drags on, but the rabbi sees he is making no headway. "What's your second request?" he finally asks wearily.

"I want my ashes scattered over Bloomingdale's."

"Why, in God's name, do you want to do that?" the rabbi shouts.

"That way, I'm sure my daughters will visit me at least twice a week."

Business jokes deal with the supposed Jewish obsession with gaining money: Jokes about materialism pinpoint their supposed obsession with spending it. Many jokes, for example, concern Jewish women's presumed preference for mink coats:

A black woman wins the California lottery and goes to I. Magnin to buy a mink coat. She tries one on.

"You look stunning," the saleslady says.

The black woman examines herself critically in the mirror. "But do you think it makes me look Jewish?" she asks.

A Jewish man goes into an expensive stationery store. "I want to buy your finest Montblanc pen for my wife's birthday," he tells the salesman.

"That'll certainly be a big surprise," the salesman says.

"It certainly will. She's expecting a mink coat."

Then there's the Jewish "pride" in automobiles:

In the 1950s, when General Motors announced, coincidentally on the eve of Yom Kippur, that it was recalling 72,000 Cadillacs, comedian Jack Benny commented: "I've never seen so many Jews walking to the synagogue in my life."*9

Most Jews unquestionably would agree with the claim of Tevye the Milkman, Sholom Aleichem's most famous character: "It's no great shame to be poor, but it's no great honor either."

The first part of Tevye's assertion, I suspect, is no longer true. For most American Jews, being poor, or even lower middle class, *is* a shame. Young Jewish adults who grew up in lower-middle-class families often relate how embarrassed they were as teenagers when attending synagogue and social functions with their more numerous and affluent peers.

The Jewish obsession with success is also reflected in the large number of Yiddish words—many of which have been absorbed into the English of American Jews—denoting either stupid people or failures: *shlemiel, shlemazel, shmendrik, shmo,* and *nebbish.*

Jackie Mason has caught the cadence of the middle-class Jewish penchant for status-seeking:

Did you ever see what happens if a Jew has a son who drives a truck? He's so embarrassed, he's hiding in Philadelphia! If you know any Jew, anyplace in the world, whose son drives a truck, say this: "Does your son drive a truck?"

"Drive! I wouldn't say he drives. He sits *in the truck. I wouldn't say he drives it. How would it look, a truck is moving, there's nobody there? So in case it goes out of control, he con-*

---

*While Benny was gibing at Jewish success and materialism, informed Jews found his comment hilarious for another reason. Walking to synagogue is exactly what Jews are expected to do on Yom Kippur, because Jewish law strictly forbids them to drive on that day. In practice, however, many Conservative and almost all Reform Jews, the only kind Benny probably knew, do drive on Yom Kippur.

trols it. He's not driving—he's controlling it. . . . That's it! He's a controller in the trucking business."[10]

In the Jewish community, "keeping up with the Cohens" can be prohibitively expensive. One frequently hears of Bar or Bat Mitzvah parties costing $30,000 or more, and weddings in excess of $50,000. Several years ago, a Bar Mitzvah in Miami achieved national notoriety when the parents rented the Orange Bowl and hired cheerleaders to celebrate the occasion.

This ostentatiousness is not without its comic side. Take this example, from Henny Youngman's autobiography:

> *A few years ago, I had just finished performing at a Bar Mitzvah out on Long Island, and headed over to the buffet. On the table was a life-size sculpture of the bar mitzvah boy rendered in ice. As I ladled fruit salad onto my plate, I heard the women behind me commenting on the sculpture:*
> *"It's beautiful," said the first woman.*
> *"It's a perfect likeness," agreed the second woman. "Who did it? Epstein?"*
> *"Don't be silly. Epstein only works in chopped liver."*[11]

Ostentatious American-Jewish social affairs were memorialized in the wedding scene from the movie *Goodbye Columbus*. But while the Jews portrayed in the film were ethnic and secular, the problem permeates the Orthodox community as well. "People often spend more in one night than teachers in Jewish schools earn in a year," a prominent Orthodox rabbi has lamented.

One reason affluent Jews throw such lavish parties—indeed, often seem to spend money so freely—may be that the Jewish tradition has few curbs to halt such excesses. Unlike Catholicism, which legislates vows of poverty for its holiest members, virtually no mainstream Jewish ideology ever exalted asceticism as a religious value. Indeed, Judaism, in its worldly orientation, aggressively encourages success. The very biblical verse that commands Jews to desist from work one day each week also insists that "six days a week you shall work" (Exodus

20:9). Throughout history, enough Jews have taken this injunction so seriously that in every society where they have not been victims of discrimination, they have been disproportionately successful. (That very discrimination induced in Jews the sort of nervousness that prompts many people to feel that enough is never enough.)[12] Jewish achievements in America have been so pronounced that Father Andrew Greeley, a leading sociologist of religion, has labeled Jews "the most successful group in American society."[13] According to sociologist Steven M. Cohen, a 1988 national survey comparing Jews and non-Jews revealed that "per capita Jewish income may actually be almost double that of non-Jews."[14] While comprising only a little more than 2 percent of the American population, Jews make up 23 percent of the four hundred richest Americans and 40 percent of the forty wealthiest Americans, according to *Forbes*'s annual survey.[15]

In and of itself, financial success does not necessarily lead to materialism, and the fact that materialism is widespread does not necessarily mean that it is condoned. In this joke, a greedy person gets her just comeuppance:

A sexy young woman walks into a dinner party on the arm of a much older man. At the dinner, the lady sitting next to the woman says to her, "That's a beautiful diamond you're wearing. In fact, I think it's the most beautiful diamond I've ever seen."

"Thank you," the young woman replies. "This is a famous diamond. It's called the Plotnick Diamond."

"A diamond with a name," the first woman says. "How romantic! Is there a story behind it?"

"Oh yes. This diamond even comes with a curse."

"A curse?" asks the lady. "What's the curse?"

"Mr. Plotnick."[16]

The real question that jokes about materialism raises is this: How is wealth regarded within the Jewish community? The answer: with great respect, provided it leads to communal and charitable involvement. Indeed, wealth plays a major, often *the* major, role in the assignment of community honors. Jewish organizations hold annual banquets to honor wealthy donors, even when other people have worked harder and contributed a higher percentage of their income.

Are Jews, then, more materialistic than others? Frankly, I don't know. There is no better answer perhaps than that offered in the old Jewish adage "Jews are like everyone else, only more so."

4

"The Doctor Is Three and the Lawyer Is Two"
Self-Loathing, Self-Praise, and Other Jewish Neuroses

▶

Self-Deprecation, Chutzpah, and the Jewish Sense of Self-Worth

Two Jews are dragged by antisemites before a firing squad.
*   The first one cries out: "Stop! Stop! You're murdering an innocent man."*
*   "Sh . . . Sh . . . ," says the second. "Don't make trouble."*

Two Jews are walking in a tough neighborhood when they spot two burly gentiles coming toward them.
*   "Uh-oh," one Jew says to the other. "We better make a run for it. There are two of them, and we're alone."*

According to Jackie Mason: "In this country, Jews don't fight. I don't know if you noticed that. In this country they almost fight. Every Jew I know almost killed somebody. They'll all tell you. 'If he had said one more word . . . he would've been dead today. That's right. I was ready. One more word . . .' What's the word? Nobody knows what that word is."[1]

Although Jews have high self-esteem when it comes to intelligence, a very different self-image prevails in the physical realm. Classic neurotic self-doubts surround anything physical, be it muscular prowess or sexual appeal. According to Jewish humor, Jews are weaker, more cowardly, and less physically attractive than gentiles. For example, in 1948, even as America's Jews took great pride in the Israeli Army's accomplishments during the War of Independence, the image of Jews as poor fighters still predominated in Jewish humor. A typical story of the time:

> *A very wealthy American Jew, potentially an enormous contributor to the United Jewish Appeal, arrives in Israel. The Minister of Tourism instructs the man's guide that he is to be taken to see whatever he requests.*
>
> *For five days, the guide takes the man all over the country. Then the American asks to be taken to the Israeli Tomb of the Unknown Soldier. There is no such tomb in Israel, so something is hastily improvised at a military cemetery. The American is brought there. But as he starts walking around the grave, he sees marked on the side, Abraham Goldman 1920–1948. He turns angrily to the guide. "I thought you said this was the Tomb of the Unknown Soldier."*
>
> *"It is," the guide says.*
>
> *"But the man's name is listed here."*
>
> *"As a soldier he was unknown," the guide answers. "As a tailor he was very well known."*[2]

The early Zionist leader Shmaryahu Levin crystalized this timid self-perception in a revealing autobiographical reminiscence. One night, during the 1936 Arab riots in Palestine, Levin was walking alone down a street in Jerusalem when he saw an Arab coming toward him. Levin lifted the flap of his overcoat and covered his face. "That way the Arab was frightened because he didn't know who was behind the coat—and I was frightened because I knew who was behind it."

Physical appearance is equally likely to evoke Jewish insecurities. Thus, the popular Yiddish expression *shayne vee a shiksa,* "as pretty as a gentile woman," makes an unstated, and uncomplimentary, assumption about Jewish attractiveness. Indeed, given the choice of being told, "You look very Jewish," or "You don't look like a Jew at all," many, perhaps most, Jews would opt for the latter. For example, David Geffen, currently the most influential figure in the Hollywood music industry, is close to many of the leading stars and moguls: According to *Forbes,* he also is one of the four hundred wealthiest Americans. Yet when Geffen, short and dark-skinned, was interviewed for a *Vanity Fair* profile, here is how he portrayed himself: "I'm just a boy from Brooklyn who wishes he were six feet tall, with blond hair and blue eyes. That's who I really am."[3]

The widespread embarrassment about physical appearance is probably rooted in the Jews' long, often unhappy sojourn in Europe. For many centuries, European Jews found themselves viciously caricatured in antisemitic cartoons, sometimes with horns and tail,[4] and invariably with swarthy features and long, hooked noses. The Jewish "shnozz" became a staple of antisemitic humor:

"Cohen won the race by a nose."

"Why do Jews have long noses? Because air is free."

Among antisemites, this negative stereotype persists. Antisemitic cartoons are still published throughout Europe, the Arab world, South America, and elsewhere, depicting Jews with grotesquely long and hooked noses.* In 1973, Yakov Malik, the Soviet ambassador to the United Nations, warned

---

*In 1913, the *American Anthropologist* published an article with the remarkable title "The Nose of the Jew and the Quadratus Labii Superioris Muscle" (15:106–108). Robert Bennet Bean, the author, believed that having large noses was so important to Jews that it determined their selection of mates. Those with the largest noses—caused in Bean's "scholarly" view by their perpetual expression of indignation—"would be selected in marriage by the most Orthodox, and would transmit a natural endowment to their offspring. Those who gave less evidence of it, might marry outside of the race." As the old New York expression has it: "And if you believe that, there's a bridge in Brooklyn I would like to show you." (See M. Hirsh Goldberg, *Just Because They're Jewish,* pp. 30–31; Goldberg's book is a treasure trove of many absurd beliefs about the Jews.)

the Israeli ambassador to stop making complaints about anti-semitism in Russia: "In my country, we have a proverb, 'If you stick your long nose into our garden, we will cut it off.'" A subsequent investigation revealed that Malik's citation of the proverb was accurate except for his obviously antisemitic insertion of "long."

Given so negative an image, it's understandable why American Jews are heavily overrepresented among those having "nose jobs." Indeed, Jews themselves commonly use the phrase "Jewish nose," and they don't mean it as a compliment.

The shame such a nose can cause can be traumatic. Famed songwriter Allan Sherman, author of the comic camp song "Hello Muddah, Hello Faddah," was rejected by a pretty girl in junior high school. She laughed off his invitation to a dance and told him that she was turned off by his hooked nose.

"From that day...," Sherman later recalled, "I felt such shame about my ugly nose that I would not sit in profile to anybody. ... If I was traveling in a bus or streetcar full of strangers, I would sit with my hand over my nose, pretending to be rubbing it thoughtfully. I had the sense of shame that I had something awful on me...."[5]

But are Jewish noses really so much more unattractive than those of non-Jews? Social scientist Maurice Fishberg actually examined four thousand Jewish noses in New York City and discovered that only 14 percent were aquiline or hooked. While that percentage might be slightly higher than the number among non-Jews, it also means that 86 percent of Jews have straight, snub, flat, or broad noses.[6]

In recent years, Rodney Dangerfield and Woody Allen have created a new genre of self-denigrating jokes. They have had a field day laying to rest the widely accepted image of the devoted Jewish family. According to Dangerfield, he was not loved even as a child. When he was born, his mother didn't breast-feed him; she said she just wanted to be friends. Another time, his parents took him to the Coney Island Amusement Park:

I got lost. A cop helped me look for my parents. I said: "Do you think we'll find them?" He said, "I don't know, kid. There's so many places they could hide."[7]

When he got older, Dangerfield did not get any more respect from his wife and children:

The other day I called home and heard [my son] say: "Mommy, it's Daddy, are you home?"

The home environment of Woody Allen, at least according to his early comic monologues, was equally unloving. On one occasion, Allen claims, he was kidnapped:

And they drive me off and they send a ransom note to my parents. And my father has bad reading habits. So he got into bed that night with the ransom note and he read half of it, and he got drowsy and fell asleep. Meanwhile, they take me to New Jersey bound and gagged. And my parents finally realize that I'm kidnapped and they snap into action immediately. They rent out my room.

In the middle of his nightclub monologue, Allen would pull out a beautiful gold pocket watch. "You should see this while I have it out. ... This speaks for breeding and it's mine. Actually, my grandfather, on his deathbed, sold me this watch."

While Dangerfield and Allen are hardly the first comedians to target the Jewish family, their jokes are distinctly different from any previously told. Traditional family humor depended on comic exaggeration of grim reality (overbearing mothers for example, see pages 27–31), while Dangerfield's and Allen's humor derives from a total rejection of reality. Indeed, if data started coming out showing major incidence of child neglect in the Jewish community, jokes about parental indifference to a child's kidnapping would no longer be funny. By claiming that their parents neither loved them nor cared what happened to them, Allen and Dangerfield are saying something that is so recognizably untrue that it is obvious their whole act is a put-on. We therefore feel free to laugh in contexts in which we might otherwise feel ourselves sadists for doing so.

But when Dangerfield and Allen start homing in on other areas of pain in their lives, they invariably draw from the traditional well of Jewish self-contempt and victimization:

My first blind date [Dangerfield recalls], I waited on the corner until this girl walked by. I said, "Are you Linda?" She said, "Are you Rodney?" I said, "Yeah." She said, "I'm not Linda."

[Dangerfield brags]: I got good-looking kids. Thank God my wife cheats on me.

[Allen remembers]: My parents sent me to an interfaith camp where I was beaten up by boys of all races and religions.

Mining the same vein, the Woody Allen character in his 1973 film *Sleeper* declares:

I'm not the heroic type, really. I was beaten up by Quakers.

And in a final burst of self-contempt, cartoonist Jules Feiffer puts the following words into the mouth of one of his characters:

I grew up to have my father's looks, my father's speech patterns, my father's posture, my father's opinions, and my mother's contempt for my father.

Jewish Chutzpah: The "Flip Side" of Self-denigration

An American-Jewish, presumably apocryphal, story:

When President Dwight Eisenhower met with Israeli Prime Minister David Ben-Gurion, the American president said at one point: "It is very hard to be the president of 170,000,000 people."

Ben-Gurion responded: "It's harder to be the prime minister of 2,000,000 prime ministers."

Jews are not known for being self-effacing. When Chaim Weizmann, a Russian Jew who later became Israel's first president, argued with some German-Jewish delegates at a Zionist congress, he commented, "You know what the problem is with German Jews? They have all the charm of Germans and all the modesty of Jews."

The neurotic self-importance that Weizmann attributed to German Jews is common among others as well; it is probably attributable to Judaism itself. Each person, the Talmud teaches, is regarded as having infinite value. Thus, "He who saves one life, it is as if he saved an entire world" (*Mishna Sanhedrin* 4:5). So seriously is this doctrine regarded in Jewish law that if one can save ten lives by sacrificing one innocent life, he or she is prohibited from doing so, since ten infinities are not worth more than one.[8]

A tradition that asserts the boundless value of each human life can easily endow its followers with an intoxicating sense of self-worth. Even *shnorrers* (Jewish beggars) are renowned for their cocky self-confidence. In *Jokes and Their Relation to the Unconscious,* Freud tells one of his favorite Jewish jokes:

A shnorrer *succeeds in getting a rich man to give him some money. Later, the man sees the* shnorrer *sitting in a very expensive restaurant eating lox. He goes into the restaurant and yells at the* shnorrer *for buying such expensive food.*

The shnorrer *responds: "When I don't have money, I can't eat lox. When I do have money, I shouldn't eat lox. So when am I to eat lox?"*[9]

A beggar with a similar worldview figures in another story, also popular among Austrian Jews in the late nineteenth century:

A shnorrer *is having heart problems and goes to a very expen-*

sive specialist. When the time comes to pay, the shnorrer *says he has no money at all.*

"So why did you come to me?" the doctor asks angrily. "You know *I am the most expensive doctor in Vienna."*

"Because when it comes to my health, I want only the best."

Judaism's insistence that every Jew approach God personally also contributes to a sense of self-importance. The New Testament instructs its adherents to come to God *through* Jesus ("No one knows the Father except the Son, and anyone to whom the Son chooses to reveal Him" [Matthew 11:27]). In the Hebrew Bible, however, God is equally accessible to all: "God is near to all who call unto Him, who call upon Him in truth" (Psalms 145:18). And while Catholics, for example, cannot celebrate a Mass without a priest, there is virtually no act a rabbi can perform for someone that the individual cannot perform for him or herself.

This feeling of having direct unmediated access to God, and the right to be heard by Him, is epitomized in the prayer of a Jewish businessman teetering on the edge of bankruptcy: "Dear God, please help me in my business. After all, You help complete strangers, so why not help me?"

In a more recent joke, a Jew with an inflated sense of self-worth meets his match:

An Israeli mayor in a small town is walking past a construction site with his wife. One of the construction workers calls out to the woman: "How you doing, Ofra?"

"Good to see you, Itzik," the woman answers. She introduces the construction worker to her husband, and chats pleasantly with him for a few minutes.

After they walk away, the mayor says to his wife: "How do you know that man?"

"We were sweethearts in high school. He even proposed to me once."

The husband laughs. "You should be very grateful to me then. If I hadn't come along, today you'd be the wife of a construction worker."

"Not at all," the wife answers. "If I had married him, he'd now be the mayor."

The wife's response recalls an uncharacteristically pro-feminist rabbinic tale. A pious couple, the rabbis relate, had been married for many years, but because they had no children, they decided to divorce. "The man went and married a wicked woman," the story concludes, "and she made him wicked. The woman went and married a wicked man, and she made him good. This proves that all depends on the woman" (*Genesis Rabbah* 17:7).

Chutzpah, one of the few Hebrew words to gain widespread acceptance in English, is the word that characterizes the self-aggrandizing attitudes in the above stories: Chutzpah literally means "insolence" or "audacity." In Hebrew it has an overwhelmingly negative connotation, epitomized in the story about a man who murders his parents, then pleads with the judge to take pity on him because he is an orphan. That joke was recalled by Israelis in 1986, after a Palestinian terrorist blinded himself when a bomb he was making exploded. When later tried by the Israeli courts for a terrorist murder he had previously committed, the man pleaded for mercy on the grounds that he was blind. The terrorist's chutzpah was in turn compounded by the anti-Israel *Boston Globe,* which headlined the incident ISRAELIS CONVICT BLIND PALESTINIAN (October 28, 1986).[10]

The same chutzpah was evidenced by Sirhan Sirhan, the murderer of Senator Robert Kennedy in 1968. In pleading for parole from Soledad Prison in 1983, Sirhan argued: "If Robert Kennedy were alive today, he would not countenance singling me out for this kind of treatment."

When Yiddish borrowed the word "chutzpah" from Hebrew, it assigned it a more positive connotation: "guts bordering on the heroic," as lexicographer Robert Hendrickson has written.[11] Alan Dershowitz, the lawyer and best-selling author, entitled his memoirs *Chutzpah*. As befits the style of the highly aggressive Harvard law professor, his book focuses on chutzpah's good side, its "boldness, assertiveness ... willingness to ... defy tradition, to challenge authority, to raise eyebrows."[12] In appealing to Jews to assert themselves more in American life, Dershowitz expresses his belief that Jews need to show more chutzpah, not less.

Chutzpah and self-denigration, it is apparent, are opposite sides of one coin, both emphasizing Jews' differentness from their neighbors. This theme runs through Jewish theology as well as Jewish jokes. On the one hand, Jews see themselves as God's chosen people; on the other hand, they believe they are judged by a severer standard *precisely* because they are chosen. "You alone have I singled out of all the families of the earth," Amos declares in God's name. "That is why I will call you to account for all your iniquities" (3:2).

Proud of their chosenness, yet aware of a history in which they have been brutalized, murdered, and repeatedly humiliated, Jews do not seem to find solace in jokes that reflect only one side of the equation. Which is why jokes that ridicule Jews and jokes that assume Jewish superiority are laughed at with equal abandon. Sometimes, both points of view combine in the same joke:

A Jewish mother is walking down the street with her two young sons.

A passerby asks her how old the boys are.

"The doctor is three," the mother answers. "And the lawyer is two."

Sex, Guilt, and Other Complications

An eighty-three-year-old man comes into the confessional. "Father," he says. "I must speak to you. I am a widower, and very lonely. Last week, though, I met a beautiful twenty-six-year-old

*girl. She really liked me. I took her to a hotel, and in the last
five days, I've made love to her fourteen times."*
    "You should say ten Hail Marys," the priest tells him.
    "Why should I do that? I'm Jewish, Father."
    "Jewish? Then why are you telling me this?"
    "Telling you? I'm telling everybody."

Jewish, particularly Yiddish, humor has no shortage of sexual material, and over the years it has proven fertile ground for
the expression of several varieties of Jewish neurosis. My
mother once bought a Yiddish comedy album and was shocked
at the vulgarity of almost every joke. When she returned the
album to the store, the owner, an American-born Jew who knew
little Yiddish, was surprised by how upset she was: "I thought,"
he said, "that all Yiddish jokes were dirty."

Many old Yiddish jokes were indeed "dirty"—frequently
more lewd than funny—and often it was rabbis, cantors, and
other respected community members who were stigmatized in
them:

*A traveler arrives in town and asks the rabbi if he can assemble
a* minyan *(prayer quorum of ten men) so he can say the* Kaddish
*for his dead father. With effort, the rabbi assembles nine, then
tells his wife to go out and ask the first man she meets to come
and be the tenth man.*

   *It is pouring outside and the rabbi's wife is a mess. She sees
a man and asks him:* "Du vilst zein dem tzenta? *[Do you want
to be the tenth man?]."*

   The man takes one look at her and replies: "Nit dem ersh-
ter afileh *[I wouldn't even want to be the first]."*

*A cantor tells his congregation's board of directors that he will
have to find work elsewhere; he simply isn't earning enough to
support his family. The synagogue's leadership tells him they
don't have the money to give him a raise, but they will help him
in other ways:*

   *The butcher promises to supply his family with meat and
chicken every week.*

   *The baker promises a never-ending supply of bread and
cake.*

  The clothing-store owner promises to clothe his whole family.

  The sisterhood president says: "I promise to sleep with you every Monday and Thursday."

  The room becomes deathly quiet. Finally, the synagogue president asks the woman why she's making such an offer.

  "I asked my husband what we could give to the cantor and he said, 'Screw the cantor.'"

These are perhaps the two *cleanest* jokes in *The World's Best Yiddish Dirty Jokes,* the most commonly available compilation of bawdy Jewish humor. It's a sign, perhaps, of some Jewish straightlacedness that the author published the book anonymously; his name is listed as Mr. "P."

American-Jewish sex jokes often turn on Yiddish words that are "dirty"; indeed, a disproportionate number of the few Yiddish words most American Jews know are vulgar, most notably *shmuck* and *putz. Shmuck* derives from a German word meaning "jewel"; in a burst either of sexual self-confidence or irony, Jews appropriated this word to refer to the penis.[13] I've always felt sympathy for people named Shmuckler, which is more or less the Yiddish equivalent of "Prickman."* The *San Francisco Chronicle* (August 28, 1987) reported a little-known episode from the Iran/contra hearings. A Lieutenant Colonel Robert Earl testified before the congressional committee that the originator of the plan to help the contras was a "General Buck Shmuck."

  "That's a real name?" asked chief counsel Arthur Liman.

  Assured by Earl that it was, Liman, who knows some Yiddish, commented: "The only guy who should have used a code name in this case didn't."

  The Pentagon subsequently stated that there was no General Buck Shmuck on active duty.[14]

  Like *shmuck, putz* has gained wide currency in English. Most Jews who use these terms are barely aware of their origi-

---

*Indeed, conservative columnist William F. Buckley once received a very abusive letter from a Dr. Prickman, to which he responded: "My friends call me Buck. What do your friends call you?"

nal meaning. Instead, they have become terms of abuse—"What a *putz*. . . . He's a real *shmuck*"—suggesting that the person being described either is a fool or a no-goodnik.

In several Jewish jokes, *shmuck* figures in the punch line, most notably one made famous by Leo Rosten in *The Joys of Yiddish*:

Mr. Lefkowitz—sixty-five, a widower—was having a very lonely time in Miami Beach, and he observed a man of his age who was never without a companion. . . . So Lefkowitz [rallied] his courage, leaned over, and said to the popular paragon, "Mister, excuse me. What should I do to make friends?"

"Get—a camel," sneered the other. "Ride up and down Collins Avenue every day and before you know it, everyone in Miami will be asking, 'Who is that man?'. . ."

So Lefkowitz . . . telephoned a circus owner, and . . . rented a camel.

The next morning, Lefkowitz . . . mounted his camel and set forth on Collins Avenue. Everywhere people stopped, buzzed, gawked, pointed.

Every day for a week, Lefkowitz rode his trusty steed. One morning, just as he was about to get dressed, the telephone rang. "Mr. Lefkowitz! This is the parking lot! Your camel—it's gone! Stolen!"

At once, Mr. Lefkowitz phoned the police. A Sergeant O'Neill answered: "What? . . . It sounded as though you said someone had stolen your camel."

"That's right."

"Er . . . How tall was the animal?"

". . . a good six feet . . ."

"Was the animal male or female?"

"How am I supposed to know about the sex of a camel?" exclaimed Mr. Lefkowitz. "Wait! Aha! It was a male!"

"Are you sure?"

"Absolutely!"

"But, Mr. Lefkowitz, a moment ago you—"

"I'm positive, officer, because I just remembered: Every time and every place I was riding on that camel, I could hear people yelling: 'Hey, look at the shmuck on that camel.'"[15]

An unexpected number of elderly men appear in Jewish sex jokes. In this case:

A very wealthy eighty-year-old man stuns his children by telling them he is marrying a twenty-five-year-old woman. The children raise strenuous objections, but the man assures them that they are all provided for, and he will do what he wants. Meanwhile, a jaded, oversophisticated friend of his has a heart-to-heart talk with him. "You know, your wife might get a little bored, seeing as how much older you are. She probably needs some company her own age. Take in a boarder, and when you get too tired, they can entertain each other."

"Good idea," the old man says.

A year later, the friend calls up to ask how things are.

"Wonderful," the old man says. "My wife is six months pregnant."

"Congratulations," the friend answers. And smiling to himself, he adds, "So I guess you took my advice about bringing in a boarder."

"You bet," the old man says. "And she's pregnant too."

Most older Jewish jokes about sex reflect Judaism's accepting, even positive, attitude toward sexuality.[16] The Bible, for example, uses the term "sporting" (*me-tza-khek*), which certainly implies a sense of enjoyment, to describe Isaac's relationship with Rebecca (Genesis 26:8). The biblical Song of Songs has some rather detailed descriptions of sensual pleasures.[17]

In the most rigorous, seemingly prudish, Orthodox rabbinical seminaries, students routinely study talmudic tractates dealing with the laws of marriage, marital relations, and divorce. The Talmud also contains folkloristic, historical, biographical, and medical material; some (admittedly very little) is quite bawdy:

Of Rabbi Ishmael ben Yossi and Rabbi Eleazer ben Simon the Talmud records: "Their bellies were so round that when they faced each another, a herd of oxen could have passed beneath them, under their bellies, without touching either of them."

A Roman matron once taunted them, saying, "Your children must have been sired by other men, for how can men with bellies such as yours beget children?"

They answered her: "Our wives' bellies are even huger than ours."

To which the Roman matron replied, "That makes it all the

more likely that your children were begotten by others."
They replied: "Love overcomes the flesh" (Bava Mezia 84a).*

Year after year, Jews attending the weekly Sabbath service
read the entire Torah, a document that is filled with frank, non-
euphemistic discussions of sexuality. For example, Jacob works
seven years for his unscrupulous uncle, Laban, to pay off the
dowry for Rachel, Laban's daughter. When the seven years are
up, he tells his uncle: "Give me my wife, for my days are fulfilled, that I may go in unto her" (Genesis 29:21)—hardly the
most delicate language with which to address one's future fa-
ther-in-law.

The Bible does not even shy away from depicting behavior
that can be characterized as bizarre. In Genesis alone, the men
of Sodom try to rape male visitors to their city (19:4–5), Lot's
two daughters seduce their father (19:30–35), Jacob marries two
sisters (29:21–30), and Judah pays a woman whom he thinks is
a prostitute—but who is really his daughter-in-law—to sleep
with him (38:15–18).[18]

Unlike Catholicism, Hinduism, and Buddhism, Judaism has
never romanticized celibacy or viewed it as an ideal for *any* of
its adherents. The Torah's *ideal* is that "a man [shall] leave his
mother and his father and cleave to his wife, and they shall be
one flesh" (Genesis 2:24).

Despite ancient Judaism's patriarchal worldview, the rabbis
regarded sexual release as no less important to women than to
men. Indeed, "a woman's [sexual] passion," they held, "is
greater than that of a man" (*Bava Mezia* 84a). In a combination
of both male chauvinism and great sensitivity, the rabbis promised that a man who brings his wife pleasure before himself
will be rewarded with male children. If he has his pleasure first,
however, his wife will give birth to females (*Niddah* 31a–b).

Because the rabbis feared that women would be too inhib-

*As to why the rabbis bothered responding to the matron's annoying and
intrusive questions, the Talmud notes that they wanted to prevent rumors
spreading that their children were bastards.

ited to initiate sexual relations, the Talmud legislated minimum conjugal obligations for husbands, based on their professions: "Every day for men of leisure who do not need to work, twice a week for laborers, once a week for ass-drivers, once every thirty days for camel drivers, and once every six months for sailors" (*Mishna Ketubot* 5:6). A man was forbidden to change his job without his wife's consent if doing so would affect her conjugal rights. In a society that permitted polygamy, this minimum schedule of relations also protected older and/or less attractive wives from being sexually neglected.

Sexual fulfillment was assumed to be so basic to a person's mental well-being that the High Priest at the Temple in Jerusalem (a position in some ways comparable to that of the pope) was required to be married. If he wasn't, the rabbis feared that his mind would drift into sexual fantasies. This fear presumably followed from the talmudic belief that great men have greater sexual appetites than their less accomplished brothers:

> *The [great] sage Abbaye once heard a certain man saying to a certain woman, "Let us arise and travel together."*
>
> *"I will follow them," thought Abbaye, "and keep them from sinning with one another."*
>
> *He followed them across the meadows. When they were about to separate he heard one of them say, "Your company was pleasant, and now the way is long."*
>
> *"If it had been I," Abbaye thought, "I could not have restrained myself."*
>
> *In deep despair, he went and leaned against a doorpost. An old man came up to him and taught him: "The greater the man, the greater his evil inclination" (Sukkah 52a).**

Despite Judaism's tradition of sexual openness and enthusi-

---

*Anthropologist Raphael Patai notes that "the rabbis used the term 'evil inclination' in precisely the same sense in which psychoanalysts use libido: the driving force behind many human actions in general. Thus one rabbi, Nakhman bar Shmuel, is reported as having said, 'Were it not for the evil inclination, no man would build a house, get married, beget children and engage in commerce' (*Genesis Rabbah* 9:7); Patai, *The Jewish Mind* (New York: Charles Scribner's Sons, 1977), pp. 498–499.

asm, what characterizes most contemporary American-Jewish sexual humor is the precise opposite: the stereotype that Jews, particularly married women, have an aversion to sex. This characteristic, along with their supposed insatiable materialism and bitchiness, is one of the features attributed to Jewish women in JAP (Jewish-American princess) jokes:

"How do you get a Jewish girl to stop having sex?"

"Marry her."

In an early skit, Mel Brooks plays a psychoanalyst who is shocked when someone explains the Oedipus complex to him: "That's the dirtiest thing I ever heard." When told that the desire to sleep with one's mother derives its name from an ancient Greek story, Brooks is relieved: "With the Greeks, who knows? But with a Jew you don't do a thing like that even to your wife, let alone your mother."[19]

Both in jokes and much popular literature, Jews are portrayed as remorseful and ashamed of their sexual desires:

"What's the definition of a Jewish porno film?"

"Five minutes of sex, followed by an hour and a half of guilt."

Near the end of *Portnoy's Complaint,* Alexander Portnoy bemoans how excessively he's been punished for acting out a few innocent and not-so-innocent sexual fantasies:

Why is the smallest thing I do for pleasure immediately illicit—while the rest of the world rolls laughing in the mud!... But me, I dare to steal a slightly unusual kind of a hump... —and now I can't get it up! I mean, God forbid I should tear the tag from my mattress that says, "Do Not Remove Under Penalty of Law"—what would they give me for that, the chair? It makes me want to scream!

It is fair to say that ancient Judaism's sexual exuberance has been transmuted in American-Jewish humor into considerable self-consciousness and guilt. No other group, with the possible exception of Irish matrons, is so often depicted as sexually uptight. This view, it would seem, has been spread into American society by Jewish comics, not surprisingly, the group that has helped disseminate the view of Jews as physically incompetent. There is no evidence to suggest that non-Jews see Jews as lackluster lovers, and it is interesting that two of the leading sex symbols in America in the last thirty years, Marilyn Monroe and Elizabeth Taylor, both converted to Judaism, while Ruth Westheimer, a Jewish psychologist, has done more than anyone since Alfred Kinsey to promote guilt-free sex.

Among other ethnic groups, sexual enthusiasm and non-stop performance are the themes around which most sexual jokes focus:

"How many positions are there for intercourse?" an instructor asks a university class on sexuality.

"Seventy-eight," a French student answers and then proceeds to enumerate them.

After he finishes, the instructor says: "But you didn't even include the most basic way, the woman lying on her back, and the man on top of her."

"Mon Dieu!" the Frenchman exclaims. "You're right. Seventy-nine."

A Russian cosmonaut returns from outer space to his village in the coldest region of Siberia. The next day, he is interviewed by Tass.

"What is the first thing you did when you came back to your house and saw your wife?"

"Better, comrade, if you ask me the second thing I did."

"What was the second thing you did?"

"I took off my skis."

Jewish men are rarely protagonists in such jokes; they are more apt to be characterized as unimaginative, unvirile, and unpassionate:

A wealthy Jewish businessman tells his assistant: "I want you to get me a six-foot blond hooker in high heels. I want her dressed in a skimpy French maid's uniform. And I want a prune Danish."

A half hour later, the assistant comes into the man's office.

"I got the hooker outside," he reports, "and she's in the French maid's uniform. Only I can't find a prune Danish anywhere."

"Ach!" the man exclaims. "In that case, forget the whole thing."

In a rapid-fire monologue of complaints, Henny Youngman exclaims: "If it weren't for pickpockets, I'd have no sex life at all."[20]

Yet I believe that the story about the potent eighty-year-old and the young boarder comes closer to the spirit of older Jewish sexual attitudes. Jewish law encourages Jews of both sexes, and at all stages of life, to continue having sexual relations. Even elderly men are encouraged to marry and, if their wives are young enough, to have children. That is probably one reason for the surprisingly large number of jokes about older men and younger women. In regard to other Jews, however, the asexual image currently seems to predominate in American-Jewish humor.

Sexual Odds and Ends

A man's watch breaks. He walks down a busy street until he spots a store with an enormous watch hanging in the window. He brings in the watch to be fixed.

The man behind the counter is a pious Jew with a long beard.

"I don't fix watches," he tells the man. "I'm a mohel *[one who performs circumcisions]."*

"Oh my God! Then why do you have a large watch hanging in your window?"

"Mister, what do you suggest I hang in my window?"

Circumcision, the oldest ritual in Judaism, dates back to the first Jew, Abraham, who was commanded to circumcise himself when he was ninety-nine years old (Genesis 17:9–14 and 24–25); later, he was commanded to circumcise his son Isaac when the child was eight days old (Genesis 21:4). For the past several thousand years, all healthy male Jewish babies are circumcised eight days after they are born. The ceremony, known in Hebrew as *brit milah,* popularly called *bris,* involves cutting off the foreskin of the penis. Although circumcision is probably Judaism's best-known ritual, one aspect of the rite, *metzizah,* is not widely known among non-Orthodox Jews. The *mohel* is expected to stanch the flow of blood from the baby's penis by applying his mouth to it. Several years ago, a friend of mine studying for the rabbinate at the Jewish Theological Seminary told me of a riddle circulating among rabbinical students:

What is the worst mitzvah *(commandment) in Judaism?*
To have to perform metzizah *on an adult male convert.*

While one might assume that there would be no parallels for a joke arising out of so obscure a religious ritual, there exists a remarkably similar American joke:

Two men go on a hunting trip. One of them is attacked by a poisonous snake, which bites him on the penis. He is in excruciating pain, and his friend runs to the nearest town to find a doctor. He describes the injury to the doctor, and the doctor tells him to go back immediately and put his mouth over the wound, draw out the poison, and spit it out. That's the only hope for saving his friend's life.
The man goes back to his injured friend, who is yelping in pain. "What did the doc say?" he asks from between gritted teeth.
"He said you're going to die."

Incidentally, since the rise of AIDS, alternate means are commonly employed to stop the flow of blood that do not involve direct contact of the *mohel's* mouth with the baby's organ.

Sign over a urinal in a bathroom at the Hebrew University: "The future of the Jewish people is in your hands."

Recent demographic studies show the American-Jewish community to be reproducing at a level beneath zero population growth. Within traditional Jewish circles, much moral pressure, accompanied by slogans such as the above, is exerted on Jewish couples to have large families.

Moses comes down from Mount Sinai. "I have good news and bad news," he tells the crowds gathered below. "The good news is I got them down to ten. The bad news is, adultery is still in."

And finally, this classic, which my wife, Dvorah, heard from Isaac Bashevis Singer:

A man, concerned about his wife's fidelity, goes away on a business trip. Before he leaves, he tells his son: "Watch everything your mother does, and give me a complete report when I return."

When the man comes back, he asks his son: "Did Mommy do anything unusual while I was away?"

"The night after you left," the boy says, "a strange man came to the house. He kissed Mommy on the lips when he came in, and they hugged for a long time."

"And then?" the man asks.

"Mommy took him into the bedroom."

"And then?"

"I looked through the keyhole. He took off his pants and shirt and then his underwear."

"And then?"

"He started to take off all of Mommy's clothes, and he was kissing her the whole time."

"And then?"

"Then Mommy turned off the lights and I couldn't see anything."

"Gott in himmel [God in Heaven]," the man says, slapping his cheek. "These doubts will kill me!"

Jewish Civil Wars

A new rabbi comes to a well-established congregation.

Every week on the Sabbath, a fight erupts during the service. When it comes time to recite the Sh'ma Yisra'el, "Hear, O Israel,

*the Lord Is Our God, the Lord Is One," half of the congregation
stands and the other half sits. The half who stand say, "Of course
we stand for the* Sh'ma Yisra'el: *It's the credo of Judaism.
Throughout history, thousands of Jews have died with the words
of the* Sh'ma *on their lips." The half who remain seated say, "No.
According to the* Shulkhan Arukh *[the code of Jewish law], if you
are seated when you come to the* Sh'ma *you remain seated."
The people who are standing yell at the people who are sitting,
"Stand up!" while the people who are sitting yell at the people
who are standing, "Sit down!" It's destroying the whole decorum
of the service, and driving the rabbi crazy.*

*Finally, it's brought to the rabbi's attention that at a nearby
home for the aged is a ninety-eight-year-old man who was a
founding member of the congregation. So, in accordance with
talmudic tradition, the rabbi appoints a delegation of three, one
who stands for the* Sh'ma, *one who sits, and the rabbi himself,
to go interview the man. They enter his room, and the man who
stands for the* Sh'ma *rushes over to the old man and says:
"Wasn't it the tradition in our congregation to stand for the*
Sh'ma?"

*"No," the old man answers in a weak voice. "That wasn't
the tradition."*

*The other man jumps in excitedly. "Wasn't it the tradition
in our congregation to sit for the* Sh'ma?"

"No," the old man says. "That wasn't the tradition."

*At this point, the rabbi cannot control himself. He cuts in
angrily. "I don't care what the tradition was! Just tell them one
or the other. Do you know what goes on in services every
week—the people who are standing yell at the people who are
sitting, the people who are sitting yell at the people who are
standing—"*

"That was the tradition," *the old man says.*

Jewish culture has long abhorred violence. (A nineteenth-
century story tells of a Jew who is challenged to a duel, is forced
to accept, then says, "But if I'm late, start without me.") Consequently, Jews generally discharge anger through verbal, rather
than physical, abuse. Jewish communal life, for example, has
long been characterized by intense, frequently vicious, and invariably neurotic infighting. Fights occur within the different denominations, between them, among Jews of different political

persuasions, even among Jews from different countries. Although the Jewish community is sometimes viewed by gentiles as monolithic (for example, in its support for Israel), Jews who know little else about Jewish life are familiar with the cliché "Three Jews, three opinions."

Within the Orthodox world, the bitterest fights generally erupt over ritual issues, and they often lead to members bolting and forming a new congregation. That is one reason there are many small Jewish communities in the United States, with one Reform temple, one Conservative synagogue, but two or more Orthodox *shuls.**

Fights inside the Orthodox world can become more vicious than the clean break of a secession, however. When the late Rabbi Moshe Feinstein, a scholar as revered among most Orthodox Jews as the pope is among traditional Catholics, ruled that artificial insemination might be permissible in certain limited instances, he was hounded by abusive phone calls in the middle of the night. In the view of the anonymous callers, any leniency concerning the use of artificial insemination was tantamount to permitting adultery, and they felt compelled to inform the rabbi of that fact at 4:00 A.M.

Obnoxious though such behavior might be, it is mild compared with the conduct of the Vilna Gaon, the greatest eighteenth-century rabbinic scholar. Himself piously Orthodox, the Gaon distrusted the Orthodox credentials of the new Hasidic movement, and thus placed the Hasidim under a ban of excommunication, thereby forbidding other Jews from marrying or doing business with them. "If I were able," he declared on one occasion, "I would do unto them as Elijah the prophet did to the priests of Baal [kill them; see I Kings 18:40]."[21]

For their part, the Hasidim called their opponents *Mitnagdim* (the Hebrew word for "opponents"; compare the Catholic Church's characterization of its Reformation adversaries as

---

*Another reason is that Orthodox Jews require more synagogues, since they are forbidden to drive on Jewish holidays and therefore need to have a *shul* within walking distance of their homes.

◀ *Rabbi Joseph Telushkin*

"Protestants"). In the Hasidim's view, *Mitnagdim* were cold-hearted, letter-of-the-law rationalists, about whom they told their own kind of hostile stories:

> *"What's the difference between a* Mitnaggid *and a dog?" a Hasid asks his friend.*
> *"I don't know," the friend answers. "What is the difference?"*
> *"I don't know either," the Hasid says.*

The fighting that goes on inside synagogues is so well known that jokes about it appear in virtually every anthology of Jewish humor (see, for example, pages 19–20).[22]

> *Two members of a congregation have been feuding for years. On Yom Kippur eve, just before the Kol Nidrei service, the rabbi brings the two men together in his office.*
> *"You must make peace," he commands. "What is the point of going into synagogue and asking God to forgive you when you can't even forgive your fellowman?"*
> *The men are both moved. They hug and promise that they will not fight anymore.*
> *When services end, one of the men greets the other. "I prayed for you everything that you prayed for me."*
> *"Starting up already?" the second man answers.*

As ugly as fights can become within congregations, the accusations hurled among the various Jewish denominations can be even more shocking. A few years ago, the student newspaper of a prominent Orthodox seminary published a column by a rabbi proclaiming: "We must oppose Reform Judaism as we opposed Nazism. We must oppose Conservative Judaism as we oppose Marxism."

In jokes told by traditional, particularly Orthodox, Jews, the Reform movement is seen as devoid of Jewishness:

> *Three Reform rabbis are sitting together, each bragging how liberal his congregation is.*
> *"On the Sabbath," the first one says, "we let people smoke during the service."*

"We're more liberal than you," the second one says. "On Yom Kippur, I announce from the pulpit that fasting is just an old custom and not required. We keep food in the back of the synagogue for those who want to eat."

"That's nothing," the third rabbi says. "On Rosh ha-Shana and Yom Kippur we have a large sign posted in front of the temple: Closed for the Holidays."

In recent years, Reform Jews have counterpunched with their own jokes against the Orthodox:

A Reform Jew goes to his rabbi, very depressed.

"My son," he says, "has become very Orthodox. He goes full time to a yeshiva, and claims that everything in our house is unkosher, so he can never eat with us. And worst of all, he's influenced our daughter. She's left the house and gone to study at some super Orthodox seminary for women."

"And what about your younger son?" the rabbi asks. "The one who was at Stanford."

"That's the worst case of all," the man answers. "He got hooked up with some Hasidim, and now lives at a yeshiva in Israel."

"Have you thought of checking your mezuzot?" *the rabbi asks.*

This joke is like the Talmud: It requires commentary. The *mezuzah* is a small box—inside of which is a small scroll written by a scribe and containing verses from the Torah—which Jews are instructed to attach to the doorposts of their house, and to the doorpost of every room.

During the past two decades, certain Orthodox rabbis have claimed that terrible tragedies ensue when Jews put up unkosher—that is, improperly written—*mezuzot*. The impropriety usually consists of a missing or misspelled word, or an erased letter. In one widely circulated story, it was claimed that after twenty-five Jewish schoolchildren were murdered by Arab terrorists in the small Israeli town of Ma'alot in 1974, an inspection of the school building revealed that twenty-five of the *mezuzot* were unkosher.

The joke in this instance, of course, is that Reform Jews are generally not scrupulous about putting up kosher *mezuzot,* in every room. In addition, the joke addresses a rarely discussed phenomenon in Jewish life, the anger and anguish many nonobservant Jews feel when their offspring turn Orthodox. The children no longer eat at their parents' unkosher homes, and sometimes contemptuously dismiss the Jewishness of their parents' lives. Such a tragedy, the rabbi reasons, must come directly from God, who is punishing the man for some serious ritual infraction—unkosher *mezuzot,* no doubt.[23]

A third type of conflict is that which occurs among Jews of different ethnic backgrounds. The tradition of disparaging Jews from other countries is an old one. For example, Jews expelled from Spain in 1492 regarded themselves, with some justification, as being on a higher cultural plane than other European Jews. In their synagogue in Amsterdam, they decreed that non-Spanish Jews had to stand behind a wooden barrier during services. In London descendants of Spanish Jews decreed that no communal charity funds be given to orphans of Spanish-Jewish men who had married non–Spanish-Jewish women.[24]

In this century, Romanian Jews somehow became stigmatized as dishonest: "What is the recipe for cake in a Romanian cookbook?" "First, steal a dozen eggs." In Orthodox synagogues, Jews put their hands over their eyes when reciting the *Sh'ma,* "Hear, O Israel . . ." The intention is to focus one's concentration on God. The story goes that in Romanian synagogues, a sign at the front declares: "We are not responsible for anyone whose pockets are picked during the recitation of the *Sh'ma.*"*

In the United States, Jews of German extraction often expressed contempt for Eastern European Jewish immigrants, whom they regarded as primitive and uncouth. In 1939, the

---

*While retelling such ethnic jokes runs the risk of spreading antisemitism, the jokes are so absurd that I hope the humor outweighs any possible offense. Anyway, I ask my Romanian-Jewish friends in advance for forgiveness.

non-Jewish psychiatrist Karl Menninger recounted how uncomfortable he felt when the owner of *The New York Times,* Arthur Sulzberger, told "a story involving the imitation of the Jewish accent of Dr. [A. A.] Brill [the pioneer Eastern European Jewish psychoanalyst] which I thought was in very bad taste. As a matter of fact, it was the second time he had told it in my presence. . . . He is such a cultivated, dignified fellow that it is amazing to hear him come out with this ridicule of the accent of other Jews." Menninger also noted that Sulzberger was "timid about being known to be a Jewish newspaper owner," and it is possible that his repeated mocking of another Jew's accent was an attempt to show the non-Jewish psychiatrist that he, Sulzberger, was a man like him and should not be thought of as a Jew.[25]

Sulzberger's ridiculing Eastern European Jews' mispronunciations brings to mind the story of a Jewish couple making their first trip to Hawaii. On the plane, they get into an argument: The woman says the name is pronounced Hawaii, just as it is written, while the husband insists that the "w" in Hawaii is pronounced as a "v." When they arrive, they stop the first person they see at the airport, an elderly man with a beard, and the husband says to him, "The state we're in now, how do you pronounce its name?"

"Havaii," the old man says.

The husband smiles triumphantly at his wife. "Thank you," he tells the old man.

"You're velcome."

Pronouncing "w" as "v" is a standard speech stereotype of immigrant Jews, but it also figures in an American joke that is non-Jewish in origin. Robert Wagner, the Catholic mayor of New York City in the 1950s and early 1960s, was a descendant of German immigrants. A popular parlor game of the time, perhaps the precursor of *Jeopardy,* consisted of a person saying a word or phrase and the other players formulating a question to which it would be the logical answer. To the phrase "9W," the name of a highway leading into New York City, the appropriate question was, "Mayor Vagner, do you spell your name with a 'v'?"*

In 1940 Democrat Franklin D. Roosevelt was running against Republican Wendell Wilkie. An elderly Jew told his friend, "I'm voting for Mendel Vilkie."

"There's no such candidate," the friend says. "His name is Wendell Wilkie."

"In dat case," the man says. "I'm voting for Rosenveld."

A final reflection on Jewish communal fights: Several years ago, a friend of mine, who had directed a major Jewish institution in California, was considering running for the U.S. Congress. He met with a powerful Democratic congressman from Los Angeles, himself a very committed and active Jew, who advised him in all seriousness: "If you've survived the political infighting in Jewish life for ten years, when you make it to Congress, you'll find the atmosphere there much gentler."

Jewish Curses†

Jewish verbal aggression reaches its heights in the variety and ferocity of its Yiddish curses:

*In German, as well as Yiddish, *nein* means "no."

†A subcategory of Yiddish curses, Jewish euphemisms, has recently been chronicled by Albert Vorspan (with Paul Kresh) in *Start Worrying: Details to Follow*, pp. 19–23. In "A Glossary for Jewish Meetings," Vorspan and Kresh note the difference between what people say and what they really mean:

"I don't question the sincerity of Mr. Stein's statement."
Meaning: "I question the sincerity of Mr. Stein's statement."
"Mr. Glasser is a most devoted and tireless member of our board."
Meaning: Mr. Glasser is a *nudnik*.
"My worthy colleague."
Meaning: My worst enemy should have such a colleague.
"I will confine myself to a few brief remarks."
Meaning: We'll be lucky to get home for *The Late, Late Show*.
"Max, our staff director, has been tireless and devoted, a giant in this field, and his contributions over the years have been beyond calculation."
Meaning: Our Max is a goner.

May all your teeth fall out, except one. And that should ache you.

May you win a lottery, and spend it all on doctors.

May you live in a house with a hundred rooms, and may each room have its own bed, and may you wander every night from room to room, and from bed to bed, unable to sleep.

May you grow so rich your widow's second husband never has to worry about making a living.

May you grow two more hands to scratch all your itches.

May you back into a pitchfork and grab a hot stove for support.

Film director Ernst Lubitsch's definition of a Jewish curse: "You should have a lot of money, but you should be the only one in your family with it."[26]

5

"Pardon Me, Do You Have Another Globe?"
Persecution and the Jewish Sense of Homelessness

▶

Antisemitism

In the late 1930s, a Jew is traveling on the subway reading a Yiddish newspaper, The Forward. *Suddenly, to his shock, he spots a friend of his sitting just opposite him, reading the local New York Nazi newspaper. He glares at his friend in anger: "How can you read that Nazi rag?"*

Unabashed, the friend looks up at him. "So what are you reading, The Forward? *And what do you read there? In America, there is a depression going on, and the Jews are assimilating. In Palestine, the Arabs are rioting and killing Jews. In Germany, they've taken away all our rights. You sit there, and read all about it, and get more and more depressed. I read the Nazi newspaper. We own all the banks. We control all the governments."*

Of all the antisemites' warped notions, the one that is most absurd is the belief in international Jewry's domination of the world. The mere fact that world Jewry was powerless to stop the Holocaust, not even politically strong enough to compel the

Allies to bomb the train tracks leading to the death camps, proves that much of the Jews' "political power" is illusory.[1] The "joke" is that the only ones who believe in international Jewry's world power are antisemites; Jews know better. As the Zionist leader, and Israel's first president, Chaim Weizmann, declared in the late 1930s, "There are two sorts of countries in the world—those that want to expel the Jews, and those that don't want to admit them":

In 1939, a Viennese Jew enters a travel agent's office and says, "I want to buy a steamship ticket."
"Where to?" the clerk asks.
"Let me look at your globe, please."
The Jew starts examining the globe. Every time he suggests a country, the clerk raises an objection. "This one requires a visa. . . . This one is not admitting any more Jews. . . . The waiting list to get into that one is ten years."
Finally the Jew looks up. "Pardon me, do you have another globe?"

Not surprisingly, the Holocaust itself stimulated bitter witticisms rather than jokes. As one comment had it:

When Hitler rose to power, there were two types of Jews in Germany, pessimists and optimists. The pessimists fled into exile, and the optimists went to the gas chambers.

And after the war:

A Jew survived the gas chambers, having lost every one of his relatives.
The resettlement officer asked him where he would like to go.
"Australia," he replied.
"But that's so far," said the officer.
"From where?" asked the Jew.[2]

As a rule, Jews have joked about antisemitism only when they were too weak to fight it. In the first half of this century, when American Jewry was politically weaker and more vulnerable to Jew-hatred, an enormous body of jokes ridiculing anti-semites circulated. For example:

During the Second World War, a southern matron calls up the local army base.

"We would be honored," she tells the sergeant who takes her call, "to accommodate five soldiers at our Thanksgiving dinner."

"That's very gracious of you, ma'am," the sergeant answers.

"Just please make sure they're not Jews."

"I understand, ma'am."

Thanksgiving afternoon, the woman answers the front doorbell and is horrified to find five black soldiers standing in the doorway.

"We're here for the Thanksgiving dinner, ma'am," one of the soldiers says.

"Bu ... bu ... but your sergeant has made a terrible mistake," the woman says.

"Oh no, ma'am," the soldier answers. "Sergeant Greenberg never makes mistakes."

A woman who speaks with a Yiddish accent enters a posh restaurant.

"We don't serve Jews here," the manager tells her.

"Dat's all right," she says. "I don't eat them."

Groucho Marx was married to a non-Jew. When their son was refused admittance to a "restricted" country club, Groucho sent the club a telegram: "Since my little son is only half-Jewish, would it be all right if he goes into the pool only up to his waist?"

Jokes like these are rarely told today by Jews, because the type of discrimination they describe generally has been eliminated. Jews can pretty much eat or live where they want and, except for a few exclusive clubs, swim and play golf wherever they wish. The first joke, which might seem to be the most enduringly relevant, recalls an era when blacks and Jews widely agreed that they had the same enemies. Today, however, the relationship between the two groups is far more tense, and a Jew who told this joke in public would risk offending blacks.

Not only has antisemitism declined in America, but when antisemitic incidents do occur, Jewish defense organizations such as the Anti-Defamation League and the Simon Wiesenthal Center respond aggressively to them. Consequently, one hears fewer jokes today about antisemites and antisemitism than in the past; people able to confront their enemies feel less need to ridicule them.

Christian Antisemitism

Prior to the Nazis, Christian antisemites inflicted the most suffering on Jews, and were therefore a favorite target of Jewish humorists.

> *A Christian and Jewish woman get into a fight in a post office line.*
> *The argument escalates, and the Christian woman yells at the Jew, "Christ-killer."*
> *"You're right," the Jewish woman says. "And if we could kill your God, imagine what I could do to you."*

Although the Jewish woman's final remark is historically wrong—it was the Romans, not the Jews, who killed Jesus Christ—the widespread perception that Jews were "Christ-killers" made them terrifying to their Christian neighbors. After all, people capable of killing God must themselves have Godlike powers; mere mortals could not slay the deity.

The belief that the Jews killed Christ also made them hateful to many non-Jews. For medieval antisemites, it was but a small step from thinking of Jews as "Christ-killers" to believing that they killed gentiles and drank their blood, or that they caused the Black Death by poisoning wells throughout Europe.

In time, the accusations became even more preposterous. In 1215, the Catholic Church formalized the dogma of transubstantiation, which holds that the wine and wafer used in the Mass are miraculously transformed during the service into the actual blood and body of Jesus. Antisemites suspected that if the wafer was transformed into Christ's body, then the Jews, having killed Jesus once, would try to do so again. From the thirteenth to the eighteenth centuries, thousands of Jews were killed for allegedly breaking into churches, stealing wafers, and "torturing" them.[3]

Another unpleasant feature of Jewish life in medieval Europe was that rabbis were forced to engage in disputations with Christian clergy.[4] The Jews hated these no-win encounters. If the rabbis argued aggressively and effectively, they were accused of insulting Christianity and were threatened with death. If they did not, they lost the debate and were expected to convert. Not surprisingly, so hopeless a situation inspired its own unique brand of humor:

In a small European city, the priest, widely acknowledged as an expert on the Bible and the Hebrew language, challenges any Jew to debate him. The disputation is to have a unique format. Each party will ask the other to translate a Hebrew term. The first party incapable of doing so will immediately be executed.

The local rabbi is terrified because he knows that the priest's knowledge of Hebrew is greater than his. The Jewish community is in a quandary; they realize that whoever enters the debate will die.

Finally, a simple Jewish laborer comes forward. "I am willing to debate the priest," he says.

The debate is arranged, and the laborer is permitted to ask the first question. "What does ai-neh-nee yoh-day-ah *mean?"*

The priest answers, "I don't know" (which is what the two Hebrew words literally mean) and is immediately put to death.

The Jewish community is greatly impressed by the laborer's ingenuity. They make a celebration in his honor, and one of the guests asks him: "Where did you ever get the idea to ask the priest such a question?"

The laborer answers: "I grew up in a village near here, and the rabbi there was a very big scholar, much bigger than the rabbi here. And somebody once told me to ask him, 'What does ai-neh-nee yoh-day-ah *mean?' I asked him, and he told me, 'I don't know.' So I figured, if that rabbi, who was such a scholar, didn't know, how could this priest know?"*

Eastern European Antisemitism:
An Especially Virulent Breed

During the past thousand years, the primary, though not exclusive, victims of antisemitism have been Jews living in Europe, particularly in the eastern part. It was in Eastern Europe that most jokes about antisemitism originated.

Ignace Paderewski, Poland's post–World War I premier, was discussing his country's problems with President Woodrow Wilson.

"If our demands are not met at the conference table," he said, "I can foresee serious trouble in my country. Why, my people will be so irritated that many of them will go out and massacre the Jews."

"And what will happen if your demands are granted?" asked President Wilson.

"Why, my people will be so happy that they will get drunk and go out and massacre the Jews."[5]

Jewish humor has long recognized that the reasons offered by antisemites for their hatred are seldom the real ones. Although no antisemite would admit that his hatred came first and the search for reasons later, that is precisely the admission that can be made, if only unintentionally, in humor.

The Paderewski joke, which circulated more than two decades before the Holocaust, proved to be prescient. A major reason the Germans built Auschwitz, Treblinka, and every major death camp in Poland was that they knew there would be little sympathy in the Polish countryside for Jews escaping from the camps. Of the three and a half million Jews living in Poland in 1939, over 90 percent had been murdered by the end of World War II in 1945.

By 1968, fewer than twenty thousand Jews remained in Poland, less than 1 percent of those who had lived there thirty years earlier. Still, Polish antisemitism did not abate. When antigovernment riots erupted in 1968, the Communist leadership orchestrated a campaign blaming Jews, who numbered less than one tenth of 1 percent of the population, for the disturbances.

For several months, the major issue on Polish radio and television and in the newspapers was the "unmasking of Zionists in Poland."[6] Small wonder that in such a climate, bitter humor abounded, examples of which have been collected in Steven Lukes and Itzhak Galnoor's *No Laughing Matter: A Collection of Political Jokes*:

Two Jews meet in Warsaw in 1968.
    "Rosenberg," says the first, "they tell me that you have lost your job, and yet you look well, happy, and prosperous. How is this? What are you living on?"
    "I'm living by blackmail," the other replies.
    "By blackmail? . . ."
    "It's very simple. There is a Polish family that hid me during the war against the Nazis."
    "So?"
    "I'm blackmailing them [with the threat that otherwise I will tell everyone that they had saved a Jew]."[7]

Not all Poles, of course, were antisemitic; among thirty million Poles, several thousand did risk their lives to save Jews during the Holocaust. Historian Yaffa Eliach has unearthed the story of one Polish couple's heroism, and the valor of a young Polish priest. In November 1942, when Jews in the Cracow ghetto were being systematically murdered, a Jewish mother succeeded in smuggling out her son to two Christian friends, a couple named Yachowitch. She sent them the addresses of family members in Canada and the United States, requesting that if she and her husband were killed, her son be sent to them.

The Yachowitchs were very devoted foster parents and risked their own lives to keep the boy alive. When Mrs. Yachowitch learned that the boy's parents had been murdered, she sought out a priest and asked him to baptize the child.

"And what was the parents' wish when they entrusted their only child to you and your husband?" the priest asked. When she told him of the mother's wishes, the priest refused to baptize the child, saying that it would be unfair to do so while there was still hope that the boy's relatives might take him.

Mrs. Yachowitch subsequently contacted the boy's family; they brought him to America and adopted him. The boy stayed in contact with the Yachowitches, and some thirty years later, Mrs. Yachowitch sent him a letter, revealing for the first time her intention to baptize him and the story of the young parish priest who refused to do so. That priest was Cardinal Karol Wojtyla of Cracow who, on October 16, 1978 was elected by the College of Cardinals as Pope John Paul II.[8]

Antisemitism and Jewish Rage

While contempt and sarcasm normally inspire funnier jokes than does wrath, every once in a while, the rage seeps through. Among the ninety-six Jewish jokes Isaac Asimov tells in his *Treasury of Humor* is one I have never seen elsewhere. It is so absurd that it is funny, yet it also reveals an intense, frightening depth of hostility to Christianity:

> *One time, young Sadie Moskowitz took her grandmother to the movies to see one of the chariot spectaculars involving the usual distortions of Roman history. The grandmother watched with a peaceful lack of comprehension until the inevitable scene in the amphitheater, where unarmed prisoners are thrown to the lions.*
>
> *At the sight of the helpless men and women facing the ferocious beasts, the old grandmother broke into loud wails, crying out, "Oh, the poor people; oh, the poor people."*
>
> *Sadie, terribly embarrassed, whispered fiercely, "Don't scream like that, grandma. Those are Christians who are being punished by the Roman government, and it's only a movie."*
>
> *"Christians!" said the grandmother. "I see." She quieted down at once. But only a few minutes passed and then she began wailing louder than before.*
>
> *"Grandmother!" demanded Sadie. "What is it now?"*
>
> *"In the corner," said the grandmother, pointing. "That poor little lion there. He's not getting anything."*[9]

The unrelieved enmity in Asimov's joke represents the flip side of a "humorous" Bulgarian proverb: "When you baptize a Jew, hold his head under water for five minutes."

When one thinks of Jewish rage against the Germans and Nazis, the late Israeli Prime Minister Menachem Begin, among the least humorous of men (at least in public), comes to mind. In the spring of 1981, when German leader Helmut Schmidt spoke of Germany's moral obligation to the Palestinian people and announced that Germany was considering selling tanks to Saudi Arabia, Begin counterpunched: "My family was murdered by the German Army," he told journalists, "and Herr Schmidt was a Nazi officer on the eastern front. How do I know that he wasn't one of the murderers?" Ze'ev Chafets, an Israeli journalist, claims that "Israelis, even many who normally cringed at Begin's rhetorical excesses, applauded enthusiastically."[10]

This sort of rage, as widespread—and usually suppressed—as it is among Jews, figures only rarely in Jewish humor about the Germans and the Nazis.*

When Jews do joke about the Nazis, contempt and ridicule, rather than rage, are the emotions that generally dominate. The pattern is broken, however, in one stunningly furious monologue by comedian Mel Brooks:

Me? Not like the Germans? Why should I not like the Germans?

---

*Even people known almost exclusively as comics rarely joke when they talk about Jewish feelings toward the Nazis. In an uncharacteristically humorless passage, Woody Allen writes of sitting in a restaurant listening to a Holocaust survivor at the next table recounting his experiences at Auschwitz. Responding to the man's seeming emotional normalcy, and reminded of Elie Wiesel's claim that concentration camp inmates rarely thought of revenge, Allen writes: "I find it odd that I, who was a small boy during World War II and who lived in America, unmindful of any of the horror Nazi victims were undergoing, and who never missed a good meal with meat and potatoes and sweet desserts, and who had a soft, safe warm bed to sleep in at night, and whose memories of those years are only blissful and full of good times and good music—that I think of nothing but revenge" (Woody Allen, "Random Reflections of a Second-Rate Mind," in Joyce Carol Oates, ed., *The Best American Essays—1991* [New York: Ticknor and Fields, 1991], p. 2).

Just because they're arrogant and have fat necks and do anything they're told as long as it's cruel, and killed millions of Jews in concentration camps and made soap out of their bodies and lamp shades out of their skins? Is that any reason to hate their fucking guts?[11]

In *The Wit of the Jews,* Lore and Maurice Cowan tell a story about Billy Wilder, the noted American-Jewish film director, who, during the Second World War, served with the U.S. Army Psychological Warfare Division:"

After the war, some Germans wanted to put on a Passion Play, and a carpenter wrote me asking permission to play Jesus. After we screened them, we found that six of the Apostles were Gestapo men, and the carpenter a storm trooper. I said. "Yes, as long as the nails are real."[12]

Antisemites and Jewish Weaknesses

Although ridiculing their enemies gives Jews a good opportunity to discharge anger, a proclivity for self-criticism is so pronounced that it even comes out in jokes about the enemies of the Jews. As one riddle has it:

What is the difference between an antisemite and a Jew?
    Answer: Ask an antisemite, "What do you think of the Jews?" and he will tell you, "A disgusting people. They care only about themselves, they cheat others in business, and they think they're better than everyone else."
    "And what about Cohen?"
    "Cohen's an exception. An honest Jew."
    "And Levine?"
    "He, I admit, is a good man."
    But ask a Jew what he thinks of the Jews.
    "God's chosen people," he will tell you. "They enrich every society in which they live. They're charitable and bright."
    "And what about Cohen?"
    "That mamzer [bastard]."
    "And Levine?"
    "A son of a bitch."

A young Jewish man comes home from a job interview.
"They did ... did ... didn't gi ... gi ... give me the job as a ra ... ra ... radio announcer," he laments. "Bunch of damn an ... an ... antisemites."

Paranoia about antisemitism is a common Jewish malady. A 1985 poll of contributors to the San Francisco Jewish Community Federation found that one third believed that a Jew could not be elected to the U.S. Congress from San Francisco, this at a time when all three members of Congress from contiguous districts in or adjacent to the city were Jews, as were the mayor and the two state senators.[13]

Not surprisingly, similar jokes are told among blacks. Jews and blacks have both suffered terrible discrimination, and both groups have members who blame all their problems on outsiders. Comedian Larry Wilde tells the story of a white man complaining to a black:

White man: *"I don't know what to do, my house has burned to the ground, my wife died, my car's been stolen, and the doctor says I gotta have a serious operation."*
Black man: *"What you kickin' about, you white ain't you?"*[14]

A Final Jewish Reflection on Antisemitism

Albert Einstein said: "If my theory of relativity is proven successful, Germany will claim me as a German and France will declare that I am a citizen of the world. If my theory should prove to be untrue, then France will say I am a German, and Germany will say I am a Jew."[15]

Forbidden Laughter: The Jokes of Russian-Jewish Dissidents

In the early 1970s, Brezhnev announces to the Politburo that he is making a state visit to Poland, and that in honor of the trip he wishes to bring the Polish people a momentous gift. It is decided that Brezhnev should bring a large painting entitled "Lenin in Poland." After all, what could be a more meaningful expression of Soviet-Polish solidarity than a portrait of Lenin, the god of Soviet communism, visiting Poland? Unfortunately, Lenin never visited Poland, and the "great masters" of the Artists Union, their minds constricted by socialist realism, can come up with no ideas how to depict Lenin in Poland.

Time is running short, and the Soviet leadership is growing desperate. Finally it is decided to approach Rabinowitz, a dissident artist. "We know you have voiced many complaints against your country," a visiting KGB delegation tells him. "But if you perform this service for the motherland, we promise you a large apartment and a lot of work."

Rabinowitz agrees to make the painting of Lenin in Poland. Three weeks later, the day before the trip, Brezhnev leads a delegation of Politburo members into a conference room. There stands Rabinowitz in front of a large canvas covered by a drop cloth. "Let us see the painting," Brezhnev orders.

Rabinowitz removes the covering, and everybody in the room gasps. The painting shows a man in bed with a woman.

"Who is that man?" someone shouts at Rabinowitz.

"That's Trotsky."

Another gasp.

"And who is the woman?" another Politburo member yells out.

"Krupskaya, Lenin's wife."

"And where is Lenin?" Brezhnev thunders.

"Lenin's in Poland."

Unlike almost all other Jewish humor, Soviet-Jewish jokes were almost exclusively directed against others; they had little to say about Jewish foibles. For dissidents it made no sense to turn such a weapon against oneself; after all, the Soviets already had the KGB, informers, guns, prison camps, and even insane asylums for sane people. The only weapon in the dissidents' arsenal was ridicule.

Humor does have a dangerous power, though. Russian satirist Nikolai Gogol noted: "Even he who fears nothing fears laughter." George Orwell wrote: "Every joke is a tiny revolution." Aleksandr Solzhenitsyn was sentenced to eight years in the Gulag Archipelago for making a satirical reference to Stalin in a private letter to a friend. As recently as the early 1970s, four university students who, as a graduation prank, placed a loaf of bread in the outstretched arm of a statue of Lenin, received long terms in a prison camp. The situation of Soviet joke-tellers did not improve until Gorbachev's succession to power in 1985.

"Lenin in Poland" made one particularly devastating critique of the Communists who ruled the USSR until 1991: Not only did they fabricate events that never happened, they also provided "evidence" to "document" them. It was not enough to claim that Lenin visited Poland, there had to be a painting illustrating the event. Just as it was not enough for Stalin to accuse many of his "comrades" falsely of trying to overthrow communism, it was essential that the accused men publicly and dramatically confess their "treachery," even though the confessions were extracted by torture.[16] This too was grist for the mill for dissident satirists:

During Nasser's reign in Egypt, Egyptian archaeologists discovered a mummy much older than any previously discovered. They were totally unsuccessful, however, in dating it. Foreign archaeologists were called in, but although they performed meticulous tests they too could not ascertain the mummy's age. A group of Russian archaeologists was called in. They too had no success, but the KGB agents accompanying them volunteered to date the mummy. Their offer was rejected; what could they know of such things? Finally, after much prodding, the Egyptians allowed the three KGB agents into the room with the mummy. An hour later they emerged. "The mummy is from 3625 B.C."

"How do you know?" the startled Egyptians asked.

"He confessed."

In addition to lies, a common target of dissident wit was the government's absurdly exaggerated promises:

"In the year 2000," Brezhnev pledges in a speech to a large crowd, "every Soviet family will have its own airplane."

"But Comrade Brezhnev," a voice calls out, "why does every family need its own plane?"

"Fool!" *Brezhnev yells at the man.* "*Suppose you live in Moscow and you hear that in Kiev they have potatoes.*"

And in a variation:

"In the year 2000," Brezhnev pledges, "Russians will go to Mars and all the reaches of outer space."
"When can we go to Vienna?" a voice calls out from the crowd.

The reign of Leonid Brezhnev (1964–1982) seems to have been the heyday of both Soviet-Jewish and other dissident humor. It was less dangerous to tell jokes than it had been under Stalin, but because Brezhnev was more repressive than Khrushchev, he sparked just the sort of antagonism best expressed via humor.

Another form of joke mocked communism's absurd inefficiencies:

A man saves up enough money to buy a new refrigerator. He goes to the appropriate office and hands over the money.
"Your refrigerator," the official tells him, "will be delivered exactly ten years from today."
"In the morning or afternoon?" the man asks.
"Why do you need to know that now?" the official asks.
"Because the plumber promised to come in the morning."

Yet another form of dissident humor consisted of riddles, in which a straightforward question was intentionally misunderstood, thereby allowing the respondent to answer truthfully:

"Comrade Rabinowitz, why were you not at the last meeting of the Communist party?"
"No one told me it was the last meeting. Had I known I would have brought my wife and my children."

"Isn't it true that both the Soviet and American constitutions guarantee freedom of speech?"

"Yes. But the American Constitution also guarantees free-dom after *speech."*

Dissident humor also satirized the Soviet people's frequent scapegoating of Jews for the daily deprivations they suffered:

At four in the morning, a line is forming in front of a meat market in Moscow. At eight a vendor appears, sees the length of the line, and says: "Comrades, we are sorry, there won't be enough meat for all these people. We have to ask all the Jewish comrades to leave."

One hour later the vendor opens a window and says: "We are sorry, but we've been informed that we will receive less meat than expected. We must kindly ask all nonparty members to leave."

When only party members are left in the line, the manager appears and says: "Comrades, now that we are among ourselves, I can tell you that owing to unpredicted circumstances, our allocation of meat has been canceled. We won't have any meat this week."

This time the people get angry: "Those damn Jews get all the privileges."[17]

Were dissident jokes all Jewish?

Robert Toth, a former *Los Angeles Times* Moscow correspondent and the man from whom I heard "Lenin in Poland," is certain that Jews created the large majority of dissident jokes. The claim makes sense. Prior to Gorbachev, most dissidents were Jews, and biting sarcasm is precisely the feature that has long characterized Jewish political jokes. In *No Laughing Matter*, Lukes and Galnoor tell this story from the early years of Communist rule:

"Standing on Lenin's tomb in Red Square, Stalin was acknowledging the acclamation of the masses. Suddenly he raised his hands to silence the crowd.

"Comrades," he cried. "A most historic event! A telegram of congratulations from Leon Trotsky!"

The crowd could hardly believe its ears. It waited in hushed anticipation.

"Joseph Stalin," read Stalin. 'The Kremlin. Moscow. You

were right and I was wrong. You are the true heir of Lenin. I must apologize. Trotsky."

A roar erupted from the crowd.

But in the front row a little Jewish tailor gestured frantically to Stalin.

"Psst!" he cried. "Comrade Stalin."

Stalin leaned over to hear what he had to say.

"Such a message! But you read it without the right feeling."

Stalin once again raised his hands to still the excited crowd. "Comrades!" he announced. "Here is a simple worker, a Communist, who says I did not read Trotsky's message with the right feeling. I ask that worker to come up on the podium himself to read Trotsky's telegram."

The tailor jumped up on the podium and took the telegram into his hands. He read:

"Joseph Stalin. The Kremlin. Moscow."

Then he cleared his throat and sang out:

"You were right *and I was* wrong? You *are the true heir of Lenin? I* should *apologize?"*[18]

Although it is often difficult to prove who initially made up a specific story, some dissident jokes were unmistakably Jewish in origin. The following, which first circulated in the West in the early 1970s, has become painfully relevant in the 1990s:

A Ukrainian Jew shows up at the office of OVIR and asks for permission to emigrate to Israel.

"Why do you want to leave the best country in the whole world?" asks the OVIR agent.

"I have two reasons," the Jew says. "When my neighbor gets drunk, he bangs on my apartment door and screams: 'Just wait until we put an end to the Communist regime: Then we'll stand up and get rid of all you Jews.' Well, I don't want to wait."

The OVIR agent smiles. "Don't pay any attention to him. The Soviet regime will last forever."

"Well, that's my second reason," says the Jew.

This last story highlights an important difference between Jewish and most non-Jewish dissidents. Non-Jewish dissidents generally focused their attacks exclusively on communism, believing that its destruction would immediately rejuvenate Russian society and propel it to a higher moral plane. Jews realize, however, that the end of communism will probably not solve the problem of antisemitism, since that sentiment is shared by many Russian non-Communists, and anti-Communists. In 1881–1882 and in 1903–1906, it was czarist officials who organized hundreds of murderous antisemitic pogroms. During World War II, many Lithuanian and Ukrainian anti-Communists actively helped the Nazis murder more than one million Jews.

Throughout the 1970s and early 1980s, Jews rarely spoke about such painful episodes from the past, especially when Jews and Ukrainians in the West marched together to protest Soviet violations of human rights. But they didn't forget about them either. In the early 1980s, Ed Koch, the Jewish mayor of New York City, was invited to be Grand Marshal of the Ukrainian Day Parade. Before starting the march, Koch said to the parade's chairman: "If we were back in the old country, I'd be running down the street and you'd be running after me with a knife." On that day, however, an event unprecedented in Jewish and Ukrainian history occurred: Tens of thousands of Ukrainians marched with a Jew leading them. As Harry Golden would say, "Only in America."

A final thought: With the collapse of communism and of the Soviet Union in 1991, far fewer antigovernment jokes are being created by Jewish dissidents. Unless a totalitarian counterrevolution occurs, one can assume that the heyday of Soviet-Jewish humor has come to an end. Thank God.

6

"And I Used to Be a Hunchback"
Assimilation and Its Delusions

▶

Assimilation

American banker Otto Kahn was Jewish by birth but had converted to Christianity. He was once walking with a hunchbacked friend when they passed a synagogue.

  "You know I used to be a Jew," Kahn said.

  "And I used to be a hunchback," his companion replied.

Jewish humor consistently argues that a Jew can never really assimilate, and Judaism agrees. According to a medieval dictum, based on the Talmud, "a Jew, even if he sins [by converting to another religion], remains a Jew."[1]

During the early 1960s, Daniel Rufeisen, a Jewish convert to Catholicism who became a monk, decided to test the outer limits of this religious principle. Rufeisen, or "Brother Daniel," as he is commonly known, emigrated to Israel and applied for citizenship under the Law of Return, which guarantees any Jew the right to become an Israeli citizen upon request. Rufeisen argued that although he was Catholic by religion, he was still a member of the Jewish people.

The Israeli Supreme Court rejected his application. A Jew who lives as a Christian, the justices reasoned, loses the right to call himself a Jew; for Jews, religion and nationality have been fused since the time of the Bible (when Ruth converts to Judaism, she declares: "Your people shall be my people, your God shall be my God" [Ruth 1:16]). One can no more be a Jewish Christian, therefore, than be a Jewish Muslim. Furthermore, although the rabbis of the Talmud would certainly have considered Brother Daniel to be a Jew, this would have meant only that if he ate on Yom Kippur or smoked on the Sabbath, he would have been regarded as a sinning Jew. They had no intention of rewarding apostate Jews with special benefits such as those guaranteed by the Law of Return.

Jewish humor, the Talmud, and Brother Daniel aside, all too many Jews have in fact successfully assimilated into the non-Jewish world, and so have become lost to Judaism. The population of world Jewry in the year 40 c.e. is estimated to have been about seven million.[2] Almost two thousand years later, the number of Jews worldwide has slightly more than doubled, despite the fact that the entire world's population is currently doubling more than once every century. While the Jews' slow demographic growth throughout history is largely due to their mass murder, it also has resulted because many Jews have assimilated.

During the past century, assimilation has been most aggressively promoted by Jews on the political left. Leon Trotsky, a leader of the Russian Revolution and at one time Lenin's heir-apparent, was born with the quintessentially Jewish name Lev Bronstein. But during his revolutionary years, Trotsky assumed his non-Jewish name.[3] In 1920, when Trotsky was head of the Red Army, Moscow's Chief Rabbi Mazeh asked the Russian leader to use the army to protect Jews from pogromist attacks prompted by accusations that they were responsible for bringing communism to Russia. Trotsky reputedly responded to the request: "Why do you come to me? I am not a Jew." Mazeh answered: "That's the tragedy. It's the Trotskys who make the revolutions, and it's the Bronsteins who pay the price." In his disdain for Jewish interests, Trotsky was paradigmatic of Jews on the far left.

Wealthy European and American Jews—politically the polar opposites of the left-wing Jews—harbored many aggressive assimilators as well, Otto Kahn being one of the more prominent examples. The Seligmans, a great American-Jewish banking family, named one of their sons George Washington Seligman, and another, Alfred Lincoln Seligman, out of fear that *Abraham* Lincoln Seligman would sound too Jewish.*

Jewish humor has long ridiculed such men as Leon Trotsky and Otto Kahn for believing that they could convince anyone, other than themselves, that they are not Jewish. In the early 1940s, screenwriter Ben Hecht approached Hollywood's leading producers, most of whom were Jews, for help in publicizing the Nazi Holocaust. David Selznick, producer of *Gone With the Wind,* refused him point-blank. "I don't want to have anything to do with your cause for the simple reason that it's a Jewish political cause. And I am not interested in Jewish political problems. I am an American, not a Jew."

Aware that Selznick was a gambler, Hecht proposed a wager. He would call any three people designated by Selznick and

---

*Stephen Birmingham, *Our Crowd: The Great Jewish Families of New York* (New York: Harper and Row, 1967), p. 150. Birmingham reports that William Seligman, the most snobbish of the Seligman brothers, came to New York from Paris in the 1870s to meet with his brother Joseph. "Joe," he told him, "now that we're getting to be men of substance, I suggest that we change our name."

Joseph Seligman nodded soberly. "I agree that you should change your name, William. I suggest you change it to schlemiel" (p. 151).

Joseph Seligman's sarcasm aside, the assimilationist process seemed irresistible, even within his own family. When James Seligman, one of the last scions of the family, died in 1964, *The New York Times*'s obituary advised that the funeral service would be held at Christ Church, Methodist.

ask them if they agreed that Selznick was an American and not a Jew. If one of them agreed, Hecht would leave Selznick alone; otherwise, Selznick would have to help his cause. Selznick accepted. The first person he instructed Hecht to call was Martin Quigley, publisher of the *Motion Picture Exhibitors' Herald.* "I'd say David Selznick was a Jew," Quigley answered. Nunnally Johnson, a screenwriter, "hemmed for a few minutes, but finally offered the same reply." Selznick's final choice was Leland Hayward, an influential talent agent. "For God's sake," Hayward snapped, "what's the matter with David? He's a Jew and he knows it."[4]

Selznick's certainty that everyone thought of him only as an American typifies assimilationist thinking. Assimilated Jews in Germany were notorious for acting "more German than the Germans." After the Nazi rise to power, Erich Maria Remarque, author of the classic novel *All Quiet on the Western Front,* emigrated from Germany. Later a Nazi leader met with him and urged him to return home. "Only in Germany," he told Remarque, "can your soul fully express itself."

"Why should I long for Germany?" Remarque said. "Am I a Jew?"

A British-Jewish joke dating from the early 1950s, when much of the British Empire had just been lost, mocks the tendency of nouveau riche Jews to deny their Jewishness.

A Hasidic Jew leaves his small town in Poland and comes to London. He immediately discards his religious garb and habits, and seeks to become an Englishman. He goes to law school and marries into a prestigious, assimilated Jewish family.

One day he gets a telegram from his elderly father, announcing that he is coming to visit. The man is thrown into a panic. He goes down to the port to meet his father and tells him: "Papa, if you show up at my house with your long coat, your head-covering, your beard, it will destroy me here. You must follow everything I ask you to do."

The father agrees.

He takes the old man to the finest tailor in London and buys him a beautiful suit. Still, the man looks too Jewish. So he takes him to a barber. The beard is quickly shaved off, and the old father is starting to look more and more like a British gentleman. But there's still one problem, the peyot, *the sidecurls around the old man's ears.*

"I'm sorry, Papa, we have to cut them off."

The old man says nothing. The barber cuts off one peya. *There's no reaction from the old man. But when he starts to cut off the second* peya, *tears start streaming down the old man's face.*

"Why are you crying, Papa?" the son asks.

"I'm crying because we lost India."

A Jewish couple—the man born in America, the woman in Europe—are vacationing. One night all the hotels at which they try to register are fully occupied. The only hotel with vacancies is restricted; it will not accept Jews.

The man says: "When we check in, let me do the talking. You don't say a word, because the moment you open your mouth they'll know you're a Jew."

The woman agrees, and they register without a hitch. The next morning the woman goes down to the pool. She dives in, but the water is very cold, and she calls out: "Oy vey." Suddenly she sees everyone around the pool staring at her. "Whatever dat means," she adds.

Assimilated Jews have been disproportionately represented among the tens of thousands of Americans attracted to Eastern religions and mysticism. It is estimated that one third or more of Americans who journey to India to study with spiritual masters are Jews. Thus, the following:

An elderly Jewish woman sets out from her home in Brooklyn for India. She travels by foot over hilltops and mountains. She crosses valleys and streams, and finally she arrives in a small rural village alongside a steep mountain. At the top of the mountain is an ashram, housing a great spiritual leader, the guru Baba Ganesh.

It takes all the woman's determination, and many long hours, to reach the mountaintop. There she announces that she has come to see the guru.

"Oh, that is impossible," the guru's assistant tells her. "Nobody is allowed to see the great guru for the next six months."

"I must see him," the old woman cries. And she sits at the doorstep of the ashram without food and water for three days.

The keeper of the gate is desperate and finally makes her an offer. "Okay, you can go in to see our leader, but you must promise to say no more than three words."

The woman promises, and the man leads her down a long marble walkway. Tapestries and flowing fabrics cover the walls. They turn into a room at the end of the hall and enter through the archway. A young man is sitting on a bamboo mat in a yoga position, chanting, "Om chanti."

The woman steps in front of him, and pleads: "Come home, Sheldon."

The attraction of many American Jews to Eastern religious groups and cults, a subject that causes considerable anguish within the Jewish community in this country, is probably due to the relatively unspiritual nature of most American-Jewish homes, and of most American-Jewish religious life. As a rule, Jews, even rabbis, rarely speak about God. In a typical Reform, Reconstructionist, Conservative, or Orthodox synagogue on any given Sabbath, the likelihood that the rabbi's sermon will be about God or other spiritual matters is small. Some Jews who hunger for a bigger dose of spirituality are attracted to kabbalah and to Hasidism. Many, however, turn to Eastern religious teachings. Some disciples have even become gurus, perhaps the most famous one being American-born Baba Ram Dass, whose English name is Richard Alpert.

The Gastronomics of Jewish Assimilation

A man walks into a Chinese restaurant.

"What's the specialty today?" he asks.

"Eggplant parmigiana," the waiter answers.

"But this is a Chinese restaurant. Why are you serving eggplant parmigiana?"

"Because this is a Jewish neighborhood."

The expression "melting pot" suggests a kitchen; no coincidence, perhaps, given that it is in their eating habits that ethnic groups most easily assimilate into American life. Among the Jews, Chinese food, followed by Italian food, has long exerted the greatest lure. At last count, there were fifty-three kosher Chinese restaurants throughout the United States, and an even larger number of kosher pizzerias. The kosher Chinese restaurants' ambience is reflected in names that synthesize their Jewish and Oriental components: Moshe Peking, Shang-Chai, and Tein Lee-Chow (*tein lee* is Hebrew for "give me"), to cite three of the best known. These are the only places where religious Jews can order "spareribs," which in kosher restaurants come from cows, not pigs.

In *Up from Seltzer: A Handy Guide to Four Generations of Jews in the United States,* Peter Hochstein and illustrator Sandy Hoffman use food to satirize Jewish Americanization over the past seventy-five years:

Jewish Dietary Restrictions:
    First Generation: Anything that isn't kosher.
    Second Generation: Anything that isn't kosher except Chinese food.
    Third Generation: Anything with cholesterol.
    Fourth Generation: Anything with meat in it, and anything that wasn't organically grown.

In another passage, the breakfasts of four generations are satirized:

First Generation: Bagel and lox with a glass of tea.
Second Generation: Bagel and lox with a cup of coffee.
Third Generation: Bagel and Nova Scotia salmon with a cup of espresso.
Fourth Generation: Two croissants, an omelette aux fines herbes, *and a glass of skim milk.*

Up from Seltzer's structure, chronicling the four-generation shift from Jewish commitment and particularism to Jewish

Americanization and assimilation, might well be a humorous takeoff on a tragic story by I. L. Peretz, one of the early great masters of Yiddish literature. In Peretz's story, "Four Generations, Four Wills,"[5] he records the last wills and testaments of one family.

The first will, written by a pious Jew, has just a few lines of text. The writer bequeaths his books to his children, asks his wife to take in a poor orphan girl, and continually invokes God's blessing on his heirs.

The second will, written by the man's son, expresses the wish that his male heirs will study the Talmud every day, and that his daughters and wife will study holy books as well. He expresses the desire that at least a tenth of his estate, and a tenth of his family's yearly income, be given to charity.

The grandson of the patriarch writes the third will. A "modern" man, his will has little to say about Jewish matters: "A telegram is to be sent to Paris," it begins, "and the funeral services are to be delayed until my son arrives." Since he has no expectation that his son will recite the memorial *Kaddish* prayer, he asks that a learned scholar be paid to do so. The primary preoccupation of the will is the disbursement of his considerable assets, accompanied by his advice on how to run the family business.

The final will, written by the great-grandson of the old Jew who was so devoted to Jewish learning, and whose primary concern was that his family lead actively Jewish lives, is a pathetic declaration: "I, Moritz Benditsohn's son, leave this world neither in happiness nor in sadness but because of emptiness. . . . I cannot live any longer, because I have nothing more to do on earth. . . . I changed peoples and languages as one changes gloves." The man signs the will, then kills himself.

Peretz was wrong, of course, in assuming that all Jews who assimilate become miserably unhappy. But he was correct in noting that when Jews stop reading Jewish books and stop giving charity to Jewish institutions, they lose their connection to the Jewish people. As Herman Wouk wrote in *This Is My God,* his spiritual autobiography: "[Jews who assimilate] . . . are lost from Judaism, that is all; lost down a road which has swallowed many more Jews than the Hitler terror ever did. Of course they survive as persons. But from the viewpoint of an army, it makes little difference whether a division is exterminated or disperses into the hills and shucks off its uniforms."[6]

When Jews Become Christians

Christ died for our sins. Dare we make his martyrdom meaningless by not committing them?

—Jules Feiffer

The Christian doctrine most unfathomable to Jews holds that Jesus' death can atone for other people's ethical transgressions. Other Christian dogmas are less problematic. For example, God could make a virgin pregnant; that would be no greater a miracle than fashioning Adam out of the earth and Eve out of Adam's rib. But Judaism teaches that God Himself cannot forgive evil deeds that people commit against others.

The belief that Jesus' death can atone for other people's sins is one reason Jews are skeptical about the theological avowals of Jewish converts to Christianity. A second reason is that Jews know that throughout history, most converts changed their faith to avoid antisemitism. One such man was Daniel Chwolson (1819–1911), one of the great intellectual figures of nineteenth- and early twentieth-century Russia. A noted Orientalist, Chwolson converted to Russian Orthodoxy in 1855 and became a professor at the University of St. Petersburg. Unlike most apostates, Chwolson maintained warm relations with the Jewish community and, on several occasions, fought against blood libels and government suppression of the Talmud. His advocacy on these issues was so forceful that according to one story:

Some friends asked Professor Chwolson why he had become a Christian.

> *"Out of conviction," Chwolson answered.*
> *"Out of what conviction?" he was asked.*
> *"Out of the conviction that it is better to be a professor in*
> St. Petersburg than a melamed [a Hebrew schoolteacher] in
> Shklop."

Chwolson's wry observation reflected the sad reality of Jewish life throughout Europe. In 1818, Heinrich Marx, a lawyer and the son of a rabbi, became a Lutheran to avoid disbarment under a new Prussian law that forbade Jews from practicing law. Six years later, Marx converted all his children, among them six-year-old Karl, so that they need never suffer from antisemitism. Ironically, Karl Marx, the grandson of two Orthodox rabbis, grew up to become a rabid Jew-hater.[7]

At about the same time in England, Isaac Disraeli converted to the Anglican church, an act that later enabled his son Benjamin to become prime minister. Unlike Marx, Disraeli retained great pride in his Jewish origins. On one occasion, when Queen Victoria asked him what his real religion was, Benjamin Disraeli reputedly answered: "In the King James edition of the Bible, there comes first the Old Testament, followed by a blank page, and then the New Testament. I am that blank page."

In the nineteenth century in Europe, Jewish conversions to Christianity were common; perhaps one third of Berlin's Jews became Christians between 1800 and 1850.[8] German poet Heinrich Heine, a reluctant Jewish apostate, declared baptism to be the Jews' "entrance ticket" to Western society. So marginal to Jewish life were many prominent Jewish intellectuals that Sigmund Freud observed: "The Jewish societies in Vienna and the University of Jerusalem (of which I am a trustee), in short the Jews altogether, have celebrated me like a natural hero, although my service to the Jewish cause is confined to the single point that I have never denied my Jewishness."[9]

In late nineteenth- and early twentieth-century America, the percentage of Jews who became Christians was much smaller than in Europe, although here too the numbers were substantial. Most Jews who converted were drawn to nonfundamentalist

Protestant denominations. Some became Quakers, leading one wit to declare: "Some of my best Jews are Friends."

Far more common, however, were conversions to Unitarianism. Because Unitarians believe Jesus to be a prophet and not God, they are the most theologically liberal wing of Protestantism. As an old American riddle asks:

When is the only time you hear Jesus Christ's name mentioned in a Unitarian Church?
When the janitor trips on the ladder.

American philosopher Alfred North Whitehead defined a Unitarian as "a person who believes there is at most one God." Although Protestant fundamentalists have long denounced Unitarians for being "heathens," in the eyes of almost all other Americans, a Jew who becomes a Unitarian is considered a Christian.

In American-Jewish humor, converts, particularly when they tried to pass as "old-line" WASPs, soon became favorite figures of ridicule:

A Jew, desperate to be admitted to a fancy country club, knows he can't get in because he's Jewish. So he converts and applies for membership.

"What is your name?" the application committee chairman asks him.

He gives one of those pompous constructions like "Hutchinson River Parkway the Third."

"And what is your profession?"

"I own a seat on the New York Stock Exchange, and I also have an estate where I raise horses."

He looks like a shoo-in for membership. "One last question, sir. What is your religion?"

"My religion? Why, I am a goy."

Jews knew that most Jews didn't convert to become Christians. They converted to become non-Jews, *goyim,* part of the majority. In a related joke:

A Jew converts to Catholicism and eventually becomes a priest. He is invited to speak in a church. After the service, the local bishop congratulates him. "Everything was fine," he says. "Only next time, maybe you shouldn't begin by saying, 'Fellow goyim.'"

The word *goy*, incidentally, is not intrinsically disparaging; it is simply the Hebrew word for "nation." In a famous biblical verse, Jews themselves are referred to as a *goy:* "And you shall be unto Me a kingdom of priests and a holy nation" (*goy kadosh*; Exodus 19:6). In time, however, Jews stopped using the word *goy* to refer to themselves, and it came to denote non-Jewish nations and non-Jews. The word also began to have pejorative connotations—in the film *The Last Dragon,* billed as a kung-fu comedy, some of the action takes place in a noodle factory named "Sum Dum Goy"—just as the word "Jew" is used derogatorily by some gentiles.* As one story has it:

A Jew converts to Christianity. The next morning, his wife sees him in the living room wearing his tefillin (phylacteries) and praying in Hebrew.
"I thought you were a Christian now," she tells him.
"Oy," he says, smacking his head. "Goyishe kop."

And in another:

Three Jewish converts to Christianity are sitting in a country club, each explaining how he came to convert.
"I fell in love with a Christian girl," the first man says. "She

*Unfortunately, as folklorist Gene Bluestein has noted, "there is no neutral term in Yiddish [or Hebrew] comparable to Gentile." Hence *goy,* with its somewhat pejorative connotation, remains the standard Yiddish/Hebrew word for non-Jew. Some Israelis use the phrase *lo-yehudi* (literally, "not a Jew") to avoid the problematic *goy.* Among themselves, Jews often use *goy* to describe ignorant or nonobservant Jews. Thus, in Chaim Potok's novel *The Chosen,* a Hasidic *rebbe* declares: "Why do you think I brought my people from Russia to America, and not to [Israel]? Because it is better to live in a land of true *goyim* than to live in a land of Jewish *goyim*" (Gene Bluestein, *Anglish/Yiddish: Yiddish in American Life and Literature* [Athens, Ga.: University of Georgia Press, 1989], p. 45).

wouldn't marry me unless I became a Christian. I loved her and so I did."

"I wanted to get a promotion at my bank," the second man says. "I knew there was no point in even applying for a higher position if I was Jewish. So I converted."

"And I converted," the third man says, "because I became convinced of the greater truth of Christian theology, and of the ethical superiority of the New Testament's teachings."

The first two men glare at him: "What do you take us for, a bunch of goyim?*"*

Several years ago, while interviewing a prominent Reform rabbi, I asked him whether the Reform movement imposed any religious standards on its members: "For example, would a Reform rabbi who came to believe that Jesus was God be expelled from the Reform rabbinate?"

"We do not expel people because of their beliefs," the rabbi answered. "In any case, a rabbi who held such a belief would effectively disqualify himself from his pulpit, and *we would urge him to see a psychiatrist*" (emphasis added).

The rabbi's last comment was telling. If a Reform rabbi suddenly announced that, as a result of reading about the Holocaust or because of terrible tragedies among his congregants, he had serious questions about God's existence, I strongly doubt that he would be urged to see a psychiatrist. To many Jews, however, any Jew who flirts with the idea of worshiping another Jew as God is undoubtedly having mental problems.

Intermarriage

A telephone rings in a house, and the mother answers. It's her daughter.

"Mama," she says. "I'm engaged."

"Mazal Tov!" the mother shrieks excitedly.

"You have to know something, though, Mama. John isn't Jewish."

The mother is quiet.

> *"Also, he's looking for work. At the moment, though, we don't have any money."*
>
> *"That's no problem," the mother says. "You'll come live here with Papa and me. We'll give you our bedroom."*
>
> *"But where will you stay?"*
>
> *"Papa will sleep on the couch in the living room."*
>
> *"And what about you, Mama?"*
>
> *"About me you don't have to worry, because as soon as I get off the telephone I'm jumping out the window."*

Until 1950, fewer than 6 percent of American Jews married non-Jews, and almost all Jews regarded intermarriage as an unmitigated disaster. Some Orthodox Jews even observed the laws of mourning for a child or sibling who intermarried. One story tells of a man who married a non-Jew, whereupon his brother sat seven days of *shiva,* mourning him as dead. On one of the days, his intermarried brother paid him a condolence visit!

Outside of the Orthodox world, however, Jews no longer tell such jokes. Since the 1970s, intermarriage rates have skyrocketed: Currently, about 50 percent of American Jews who marry are choosing non-Jewish spouses.[10] While this statistic has received much publicity, few Jews realize that a high level of intermarriage is not unique to the United States nor even to the current era. In pre-Holocaust France and Germany, intermarriage rates also approached 50 percent within three generations of the Jews being "emancipated" (receiving basic civil rights).

The United States, and a few other English-speaking countries, such as Canada, Australia, and South Africa, were long the exceptions in their low levels of intermarriage. This was not because most American Jews were pious; in fact, the overwhelming majority were not. Rather, it was that people raised in Yiddish-speaking homes—as most first-generation American Jews were—*even* if the homes were nonreligious, were unlikely to feel so socially at ease with non-Jews that they would marry them.

By the 1970s and 1980s, however, the large majority of young Jewish adults had been raised by American-born parents in English-speaking homes. Their entire lives had been spent mixing with non-Jews, and they felt fully comfortable being with them. It is hardly surprising, therefore, that intermarriage rates started rising dramatically. But although American intermarriage rates rival those of nineteenth-century Western Europe, there is one important difference concerning their repercussions. In France and Germany, when Jews intermarried, either the Jewish partner converted to Christianity or agreed that the children be raised as Christians. In America, when an intermarriage occurs, the couple usually agrees to expose the children to both religions. When a conversion does take place, however, it is more likely to be of the non-Jewish spouse to Judaism than the reverse. For this reason, intermarriage is not necessarily as much of a "death knell" to American Jewry as it was to European. Nonetheless, within the past two decades, the percentage of non-Jews converting to Judaism has declined markedly. In intermarriages that occurred before 1965, 20 percent of the non-Jews converted; since 1985 only 10 percent have done so.[11]

Many conversions to Judaism are done haphazardly and with unbecoming speed—one Miami rabbi used to advertise regularly that if you came into his office as a non-Jew at 9:00 A.M., you could emerge as a fully converted Jew by 5:00 P.M. In recent years, and in all three major denominations of Judaism, the number of non-Jews interested in seriously embracing Judaism—as opposed to those whose conversions are triggered by the desire to spare their Jewish in-laws heart attacks—has increased dramatically. This phenomenon has even influenced the type of jokes Jews tell about intermarriage.

Because the following joke requires using a word that Jews should never use, *shiksa*, it demands a brief introduction. Most Jews think that *shiksa* means "female gentile" and *shaygetz*, "male gentile." (One joke has it that the two winemakers Manischewitz and Christian Brothers merged to form a new company called Manishaygetz.) However, *shiksa* literally means "female abomination," and *shaygetz* "male abomination." While few Jews know that this is what these words actually mean, they should have guessed that they are offensive. After all, if you're speaking in one language, and refer to a member of a different group in another, you're probably not using a term of endearment. But since the word is indispensable to the following joke, feel free to use it—just this once:

> *A Jewish boy is going off to college and his father says to him: "Look, we've never been a religious family, so I'm not expecting you to become suddenly religious. But promise me one thing: You won't marry a* shiksa."
>
> *The boy promises.*
>
> *Sure enough, his senior year he falls in love with a non-Jewish girl. She loves him too, but he tells her he can't marry her because she's not Jewish.*
>
> *"Don't worry," she says. "I'll convert."*
>
> *After serious study, the girl converts. They marry and go off on their honeymoon. Four weeks later, Saturday morning at 9:00* A.M., *the doorbell rings in their house. It's the boy's father. He's very upset. "You know that the last Saturday of every month we go over the books at the office. Why didn't you come down?"*
>
> *"I couldn't come," the boy says. "My wife says it's forbidden. It's Shabbat."*
>
> "I told you not to marry a shiksa," *the father screams.*[12]

The irony is profound. In many contemporary American-Jewish families, it's the convert to Judaism who takes religion seriously, only to find that the Jewish family into which he/she has married disdains or even ridicules the person's religiosity.

Shlomo Riskin, a prominent Orthodox rabbi in New York and Israel, tells of a very committed non-Jewish woman whom he converted to Judaism, who shortly thereafter became nonobservant. Riskin soon learned that not only did her husband's family refuse to practice any of the rituals she had learned, they also told her repeatedly that there was no reason for her to practice them either. "I learned an important lesson from that case," Rabbi Riskin said. "Whenever you teach conversion classes to a non-Jew who is involved with a Jew, it is vital that their Jewish boyfriend or girlfriend come with them to all the classes. Because the sort of Jew who is most apt to intermarry is often as unknowledgeable about Judaism as is the non-Jewish partner, and needs the conversion classes every bit as much."

Today, most American-Jewish leaders would maintain, it is intermarriage, not antisemitism, that threatens American Jewry's future viability. As Milton Himmelfarb has quipped:

*What do you call the grandchildren of intermarried Jews? Christians.**

---

*Himmelfarb's sally is a reworking of a mordant response to the age-old question: "Who is a Jew?" The answer: "One who will have Jewish grandchildren."

7

"If I Could Just See One Miracle"
Poking Fun at God, His Law, and His
Spokesmen on Earth

▶

Is God an Underachiever?

A man brings some very fine material to a tailor and asks him to make a pair of pants. When he comes back a week later, the pants are not ready. Two weeks later, they still are not ready. Finally, after six weeks, the pants are ready. The man tries them on. They fit perfectly. Nonetheless, when it comes time to pay, he can't resist a jibe at the tailor.

"You know," he says, "it took God only six days to make the world. And it took you six weeks to make just one pair of pants."

"Ah," the tailor says. "But look at this pair of pants, and look at the world!"

Jokes aimed at God tend to be the gentlest in the Jewish tradition—ironic digs, rather than belly laughs. More than any other contemporary comedian, Woody Allen is the master of this genre: "If only God would give me a clear sign of His existence. Like making a large deposit in my name in a Swiss bank account."[1] In Allen's film *Love and Death,* the character of Boris

Grushenko mines the same vein: "If I could just see a miracle. Just one miracle. If I could see a burning bush, or the seas part, or my Uncle Sasha pick up a check." Elsewhere, Allen makes a simple commonsense appeal to God: "I don't want to achieve immortality through my work; I want to achieve it by not dying."[2]

The disparity between God's perfection and the imperfection of the world He created inspires much of the humor about God. Indeed, the complaining spirit that runs through many anti-God jokes and witticisms is, in part, rooted in the Bible and other Jewish holy writings. Although the Bible contains little humor, it has plenty of complaints, and it's only a short step from a *kvetch* to a joke. "Awake, why do you sleep, O Lord?" the Psalmist cries out (Psalms 44:23–25), in protest at God's seeming indifference to the Jews' sufferings and oppression.

Hundreds of years later, in a passage of unparalleled bitterness, the Talmud records the reaction of the School of Rabbi Ishmael to God's silence during the Roman destruction of Jerusalem: "Who is like You among the dumb?" (*Gittin* 56b). The question "God, why do You permit the righteous to suffer and the wicked to prosper?" seems to lie at the root of almost all the biblical and rabbinic complaints.

No Jewish text has ever answered this question satisfactorily, although the prophets repeatedly insist that *because* God is good, justice will one day triumph. Contemporary Jews, most of whom lack the prophets' religious faith, do not usually find this response consoling. Countering the comforting cliché that good people have at least one advantage over the wicked, they sleep better at night, Woody Allen notes: "But the wicked seem to enjoy their waking hours more."

A statement made by a Hasidic *rebbe* in Auschwitz is as bitter as the Talmud, and more biting than Woody Allen: "There is a possibility that the Master of the Universe is a liar," he told his followers.

Shocked at this heresy, the *rebbe*'s listeners asked: "How can that be?"

"Because," the *rebbe* answered, "when God looks down from heaven at what is going on here, He says, 'I am not responsible.' And that is a lie." In other words, because God gave man free will, He bears responsibility for mankind's terrible misuse of it.*

While there is an obvious, and logical, response to the *rebbe*'s accusation of God—human beings have free will; therefore, if they act evilly, it is their fault, not God's—a question persists: Why did God create many human beings who are drawn to sadistic violence? Certainly, He could have endowed man with free will without making such horrible traits so appealing to some people. Nazis, in other words, might be wholly guilty of their actions, but that does not mean that God is totally free of responsibility. As Woody Allen has put it (in *Love and Death*): "If it turns out there is a God, I don't think He is evil. I think that the worst thing that you can say about Him is that He is an underachiever."

> *A reporter, interviewing Rabbi Seligman after a bolt of lightning had struck the synagogue roof and sent it crashing down into ruins, asked, "Rabbi, what was your reaction when you saw this terrible devastation?"*
>
> *"My first reaction?" The rabbi chuckled. "I thought, thank goodness, we took out insurance against acts of God."*[3]

The belief in chosenness causes most Jews to assume that God has a warm spot for them in His heart. On this planet, however,

---

*To contend, as the *rebbe* does, that God bears responsibility for human evil, is to come perilously close to adopting the reasoning of Dr. Robert Servatius, Adolf Eichmann's defense lawyer. Aware that there was not much to be said on behalf of a man who supervised the murder of six million people, Servatius opted for a theological defense. The Jews, he argued before the Israeli court trying Eichmann, are God's chosen people. Does not the fact that God allowed so many of them to be killed mean that the Holocaust must have been His will? Why therefore punish Eichmann for carrying out what God wanted? Needless to say, the Israeli court was not convinced. While few Jews were impressed with Servatius's argument on behalf of Eichmann, few are unmoved by the *rebbe*'s bitter charge against God.

the existence of this warm spot, for Jews or anyone else, is far less apparent. Indeed, a series of Yiddish sayings suggests that God can be capricious. *Mann trakht und Gott lakht,* runs the most famous, "Man makes plans [literally thinks] and God laughs." And Woody Allen has cynically defined Yom Kippur as the "sacred holiday commemorating God's reneging on every promise."

In the guise of pious wonder stories, one even finds talmudic folktales poking fun at God's capriciousness. In one of these tales, set in the first century B.C.E., a terrible drought has befallen Israel, and "the people sent a message to Honi the Circle Drawer [a well-known saint and miracle-worker]: 'Pray that rain may fall.' [Honi] prayed and no rain fell. He thereupon drew a circle and stood within it.... He exclaimed [before God]: 'Master of the Universe, Your children have turned to me because [they believe] me to be a member of Your house. I swear by Your great name that I will not move from here until You have mercy upon your children.'"

God's response?

"Rain began to drip down and [Honi's] disciples said to him: 'We look to you to save us from death' [i.e., such a drizzle won't help us at all]. ... Thereupon, he exclaimed: 'It is not for this that I have prayed, but for rain [to fill] cisterns, ditches, and caves.'"

Now that Honi has made it clear to God what is needed, does the Lord send an appropriate response? No.

"The rain then began to come down with great force, every drop being as big as the opening of a barrel, and the sages estimated that no drop was less than [the equivalent of the contents of six eggs].

"His disciples then said to him: 'Master, we look to you to save us from death, we believe that the rain [now falling] came down to destroy the world.'

"Thereupon, he exclaimed before [God], 'It is not for this that I have prayed, but for rains of benevolence, blessing and bounty.'

"Then rain fell normally" (*Ta'anit* 23a).

Does not this talmudic tale suggest that God is the primordial joker? Only when He has "used up his tricks," a drizzle and then a deluge, does God send the kind of rain that He knows the Jews needed all along.

The Messiah

In a small Russian shtetl, the community council decides to pay a poor Jew a ruble a week to sit at the town's entrance and be the first to greet the Messiah when he arrives.

The man's brother comes to see him, and is puzzled why he took such a low-paying job.

"It's true," the poor man responds, "the pay is low. But it's a steady job."

The concept of a messiah is one of Judaism's major contributions to Western thinking, and lies at the heart of Christianity. Because the messianic prophecies of world peace and redemption were not fulfilled in Jesus' time, Jews reject Christianity's messianic claims.

For the Jews, the Messiah's arrival lies in the future. In the twelfth and most famous of his Thirteen Articles of Faith, Maimonides wrote: "I believe in the coming of the Messiah, and though he tarry, I will wait for him on any day on which he comes." During the Holocaust, countless Jews sang these words on their way to the gas chambers.

Among many Orthodox Jews, the Messiah's coming is regarded as an ever-present possibility. When the nineteenth-century Hasidic *rebbe* Levi Yitzchak of Berditchev sent out invitations to his son's wedding, he wrote that it would take place in Jerusalem on such-and-such a date and time, but "if, God forbid, the messiah has not yet arrived, then the wedding will be held on the same date and time here in Berditchev."

Despite Judaism's fervent anticipation of the Messiah's

arrival, history has taught Jews to be skeptical about predictions that it is imminent, for they have had too many bad experiences with putative messiahs.[4] In the first century, Rabban Yochanan ben Zakkai taught: "If you should happen to be holding a sapling in your hand when they tell you that the messiah has arrived, first plant the sapling, then go and greet the messiah."[5] Less than a century later, after Rabbi Akiva urged Jews to follow the would-be Messiah Simeon Bar-Kokhba, Rabbi Yochanan ben Torta prophesied to him: "Grass will grow out of your cheekbones, and the messiah still will not have arrived."[6] In the twelfth century, Moses Maimonides counseled Yemen's Jews not to waste their time in mystical speculations concerning the date of the Messiah's arrival.

There is reason to believe that many Jews in Yemen failed to follow Maimonides's counsel. According to one medieval folktale, two men arrived in a Yemenite town and told the inhabitants that the Messiah was arriving that night and would transport them all to Israel. The people were instructed to remain on their roofs the entire night, but the Messiah did not come. In the morning, when they went down from the roofs, the strangers were gone—as well as the townspeople's possessions.

The bitterness engendered by false messiahs has not gone unnoticed in Jewish humor:

A Jew comes home from synagogue and tells his wife: "They say the Messiah is coming any day, and will take us all to Israel."

The wife becomes hysterical. "Oh no! It would be terrible. It took years till we could finally move into this neighborhood, and buy the house we wanted. Now we've spent a fortune fixing it up. I don't want the Messiah to take us away."

"Okay, okay, don't worry," the husband says. "We survived Pharaoh, we survived Haman. With God's help, we'll survive the Messiah too!"

The conflict between Judaism's optimistic assertion that the Messiah is coming and the world will be perfect (*tikkun olam*) and the Jewish people's experience of oppression engendered just the sort of skepticism in which humor flourishes. If things are really *this* bad, more than a few Jews thought, are they really going to get *that* good? To the prophets, the answer is an unequivocal yes. According to Isaiah, a wonderful future is coming. Jews will be restored to their own, independent homeland, and there will be world peace: "Nation shall not lift up sword against nation, neither shall they learn war anymore" (Isaiah 2:4). He even prophesies changes in the character of animals: "And the calf and the lion shall lie down together, and none shall be afraid" (11:6). So utopian a prediction could hardly escape the scalpel of Jewish wit. According to Woody Allen, the prophecy should have read: "The lion and the calf shall lie down together but the calf won't get any sleep."[7]

Or, as one final joke has it:

A man visits a zoo and is taken to the lion's cage. He witnesses there the literal fulfillment of Isaiah's prophecy—a lion and a calf in a cage together.

Amazed, he calls over an attendant. "How long have you had a lion and a calf in a cage together?"

"Over a year already."

"How do you do it?"

"It's easy. Every morning we put in a new calf."

Rabbis

A rabbi suffers a severe heart attack and is confined to the hospital for several weeks. The synagogue's president pays him a visit.

"I want you to know, Rabbi, that last night the board of directors voted a resolution wishing you a speedy recovery. And it passed, twelve to nine."

Until modern times, rabbis were the scholars, leaders, and most respected members of the Jewish community. Write down the names of prominent Jews between the first century and the seventeenth century, and rabbis such as Hillel, Akiva, Rashi, and Maimonides will probably dominate the list. In the Jewish folklore of that period, rabbis were the dominant characters, and, almost invariably, they were depicted either as heroes or as brilliant men, or both.

In one characteristic medieval folktale, a rabbi's wisdom saved the entire community of Seville, Spain, from death. Along with other leading Jews, he had been arrested after being accused by a powerful priest of murdering a Christian child and using the dead boy's blood in a religious ritual (an accusation known as the "blood libel"). The priest piously declared that the Jews would be tried by God, not him. He would simply fold two pieces of paper and put them in a hat; one would read "Innocent," the other "Guilty." The rabbi was to choose one of the pieces of paper. If the one he extracted read "Innocent," he and the other Jews would be released. If it read "Guilty," all of Seville's Jews would be burned.*

The hat was placed in front of the rabbi.

"At least there's a fifty percent chance you will choose 'Innocent,'" one man whispered to the rabbi.

The rabbi knew, however, that there really was no chance at all. The priest would not run the risk that either chance or God would save the Jews; both pieces of paper undoubtedly had the same word on them: "Guilty."

"Choose already," the priest commanded.

The rabbi quickly pulled out a piece of paper, put it in his mouth, and swallowed it.

"What have you done?" the priest cried out. "How will we know which paper you swallowed?"

*The Jews knew that the priest wasn't making an idle threat. In one famous case, in England in 1255, nineteen Jews were hanged for "ritually" killing Hugh of Lincoln, a Christian boy who had actually drowned in a cesspool.

"Look at the one which is still in the hat," the rabbi said. "Whatever it reads, I swallowed the opposite."[8]

Such are the rabbis of Jewish folklore, although the vision of the rabbi as the all-wise leader still persists among the Hasidim and many other Orthodox Jews.[9] Hasidic Jews, in particular, regard telling stories about saintly and wise rabbis as a religious act, and compilations of such stories are eagerly consumed. Many of these tales have become known to non-Hasidim through Martin Buber's two-volume collection, *Tales of the Hasidim.*

The late Rabbi Shlomo Zevin published a collection of hundreds of Hasidic stories. My favorite concerns Rabbi Israel of Vishnitz, who used to take a nightly stroll with his *gabbai* (assistant). One evening, the *rebbe* stopped by the house of one of the wealthiest Jews in Vishnitz, the director of the local bank.

"Let us go inside," the *rebbe* said.

The *gabbai* was puzzled. The bank director was known to be a secular Jew, anything but a follower of the *rebbe.* He could not imagine what business the *rebbe* had in such a house.

The *gabbai* knocked on the door, and when the director of the bank opened it, he invited the men inside. The *rebbe* sat down, the director waited for him to speak, but the *rebbe* said nothing. The bank director knew that protocol demanded that he not question the *rebbe* directly, so he turned to the *gabbai,* who simply shrugged his shoulders; there was nothing he could tell the man.

After twenty minutes of silence, the *rebbe* stood up. "*Shalom aleikhem* [Good-bye]," he called to the bank director as he started toward the front door.

The man could no longer restrain his curiosity. "Why did you come here, Rabbi?" he asked.

"To perform a *mitzvah* [commandment]."

"What *mitzvah* is that?"

"It says in the Talmud that just as you are required to re-prove somebody if you feel that your reproof will be heeded, so too are you required to keep silent if you know that your reproof will be ignored. Now what kind of *mitzvah* would I be performing if I just sat in my own house and was silent? No, I knew that I had to go to the house of the person who would not listen to the reproof and sit there quietly and not offer it. So I came here to perform that *mitzvah*."

"And perhaps," the bank director said, "I *will* listen."

"I'm afraid you won't," the *rebbe* said.

The more the *rebbe* refused to express his reproof, the more the bank director was consumed with curiosity. "You must tell me!" the man finally cried out in desperation. "Perhaps I will listen."

"You know, of course, so-and-so," the *rebbe* finally said, mentioning the name of a widow in the town. "She has not been able to make her mortgage payments, and you have sent her a notice that your bank will repossess her house."

"Oh that," the director said, shrugging off the story. "It has nothing to do with me. I am not the owner of the bank, just the director. I don't have the right to forgive a loan, it's not my money. There is nothing I can do."

"It's exactly as I said," the *rebbe* said. "You would not listen."

And he walked away without saying another word.

The bank director did not sleep that night. The next morning, he paid the widow's mortgage out of his own pocket.[10]

A more recent story features Rabbi Israel Meir Kagan (who died in Poland in 1933), who was known throughout the Jewish world as the *Haffetz Hayyim* ("Lover of Life"). In addition to being a first-rate scholar, the *Haffetz Hayyim* was known to be a saint. His most famous book was an appeal to Jews not to engage in talebearing.

Once, one of his students was arrested and falsely accused

of a crime. The defense lawyer summoned the elderly rabbi as a character witness.

Before the *Hafetz Hayyim* testified, the defense lawyer tried to impress the judge with the rabbi's saintliness.

"Do you know what the Jews say about him?" he said to the judge. "That one day he came home and found a thief ransacking his house. When the thief, who was still clutching some money and other items, saw the rabbi he ran out of the house. And the rabbi ran after him, shouting, 'I declare all of my property ownerless' [so that the thief would not be guilty of stealing anything]."

The judge peered down at the defense lawyer skeptically. "Do you believe that really happened?" he asked.

"I don't know, Your Honor," the lawyer said. "But they don't tell stories like that about you or me."

In addition to saintliness, Hasidic *rebbes* in particular have been heralded for possessing keen wit:

Rabbi Shmuel of Sokotchov complained once to his father that the constant stream of visitors to see him was depriving him of time to study.

His father advised him: "If they are wealthy, ask them for a loan—and you will never see them again. If they are poor, give them a loan—and you will never see them again."

In the mid-1980s, a Hasidic rebbe *was asked his opinion of the Iran-Iraq war.*

"I wish both sides Mazal Tov!" *the* rebbe *answered.*

Some one million people died in the eight-year war between Iran and Iraq, so the *rebbe*'s response sounds heartless. But given that both Iran and Iraq were committed to destroying Israel (indeed, Iraq has long been trying to procure an atom bomb to ensure her destruction), the *rebbe*'s wish becomes a bit more understandable.

The Rough World of American Rabbis

It is no coincidence that many of the foregoing stories originate overseas, and have as their heroes highly traditional Eastern European rabbis. The rabbis who inhabit modern Jewish humor are of a different breed. They may be bright or they may not be, but one thing is certain: venerated they are not.

Richard Rubenstein, a professor of religion and an ordained Conservative rabbi—he has the unusual distinction of also having studied at Reform and Orthodox seminaries—wrote a fascinating essay, "A Rabbi Dies," in which he offers some insights as to why synagogue boards, particularly Conservative ones, often torment their rabbis. On the one hand, Rubenstein observes, lay leaders perceive the rabbi as a religious and moral authority whom they should revere; on the other, it is difficult for them to experience much reverence toward a person whom they hire and fire and who must apply to them for every raise. Rubenstein describes one particular synagogue in Pennsylvania where "the trustees' attitude toward [the] rabbi vacillated between inordinate respect for someone who took the place of their fathers, and contempt for the valet."[11]

Contemporary Jews' "reverence" toward their rabbis has led to jokes like this one:

> *"My rabbi is so brilliant," a Jew brags to a friend, "that he can speak for an hour on any topic."*
>
> *"And my rabbi is so brilliant," the friend responds, "that he can speak for two hours on no topic."*

Rabbis who talk too much are often ridiculed in Jewish life. Joseph Lookstein, an extremely successful pulpit rabbi, used to warn seminary students at Yeshiva University: "If you haven't struck oil after twenty minutes, stop boring."

Modern Jewish humor commonly indicts rabbis, once the guardians of the Jewish soul, for false humility as well as verbosity:

In a large congregation on Yom Kippur, the cantor stands up to start the service. Suddenly he is overcome with trepidation. He runs over to the Ark, where the Torah scrolls are kept, and speaks aloud to God: "Lord, I am not worthy to lead this holy congregation in prayer. What am I but dust and ashes?"

The rabbi is deeply touched by the cantor's words. He too runs to the Ark and cries out to God: "I am nothing in Your eyes. What have I ever done that is worthy?"

At this point, the shammes *is also moved. He bounds up from his seat, runs to the Ark, and calls out: "God, I am a man of no value, a miserable sinner, a nothing."*

The rabbi taps the cantor on the shoulder. "Now look who's calling himself a nothing?"

In clerical jokes, "Orthodox rabbi" is a code phrase describing a man who is pious and unworldly; "Reform rabbi" means a man—there aren't yet many jokes about women rabbis—who is Jewishly ignorant and assimilated.

A newly rich Jewish businessman buys a Jaguar and brings it to an Orthodox rabbi for a brakha *(blessing). The rabbi has no idea what a Jaguar is and sends the man away.*

He brings the car to a Reform rabbi. The rabbi is very well aware what a Jaguar is, but has no idea what a brakha *is.*

Because extremes are what work in humor, there are not many jokes about Conservative rabbis. One of the few that exist highlights Conservatism's "middle"—some would say "muddled"—ideological position between the two other major Jewish denominations:

Orthodox rabbis always wear a yarmulka. Reform rabbis never do. Conservative rabbis keep their yarmulka in their pockets.

Jokes about cantors, a subgenre of rabbi jokes, often focus on their supposed vanity and their possession of voices that lack the quality of, say, Luciano Pavarotti's:

A cantor brags before his congregation in a booming, bellowing voice: "Two years ago I insured my voice with Lloyds of London for $750,000."

There is a hushed and awed silence in the crowded room. Suddenly, from the back, the quiet, nasal voice of an elderly woman is heard, "So what did you do with the money?"

A man was hired to serve as the extra rabbi for a Conservative congregation's overflow service on Rosh ha-Shana and Yom Kippur. "You must be aware of one thing," the senior rabbi told the newcomer. "Our cantor has a big ego and refuses to permit us to hire a second cantor. Therefore, the cantor prays with one congregation and his voice is piped into the other. We must make sure, therefore, that our sermons are of the exact same length. On the second day of Rosh ha-Shana, the cantor is praying with your congregation. I have prepared a thirty-two-minute sermon. Make sure you do the same."

The man went home and prepared a thirty-two-minute sermon. But when he checked his self-winding watch in the middle of his speech, he saw that it had stopped running. Nonetheless, knowing that he had prepared a thirty-two-minute speech, he finished the talk as he had prepared it and signaled to the cantor, who immediately began chanting, "Yitgadal ve-yitkadash," the Kaddish prayer that inaugurates the important prayers in the service and is also the memorial prayer for the dead.

Unfortunately, the new rabbi's nervousness caused him to deliver a thirty-two-minute sermon in twenty-six minutes.

Five minutes later, the senior rabbi came running in, yelling, "You made a fool out of me in front of my entire congregation."

"Wh . . . what happened?" the new rabbi stammered.

"I had just reached the emotional high point of my speech. I was saying: 'Today there are those who say that God is dead. Is God dead? And the cantor started Yitgadal ve-yitkadash.'"

A cantor applies for a position at a synagogue and lists the congregations where he has worked previously. The synagogue's president contacts his counterpart at one of the congregations for a reference. The man writes back: "This cantor is like Abraham, like Moses; indeed, he is like an angel."

The president immediately hires the cantor, but when he comes to the synagogue that Shabbat, catastrophe ensues. The cantor's voice warbles, he is arrogant, and everyone is very disappointed.

Monday morning, the president makes a furious call to the man who had written him the letter of recommendation. "How

*could you dare tell me that he was like Abraham, Moses, and
an angel? He was horrible."*

*"Everything I said is absolutely true," the man insists. "Abra-
ham couldn't sing, and this cantor can't sing. Moses stuttered
(Exodus 4:10), and this cantor stutters. An angel isn't a* mensch
[a human being], and this cantor isn't a mensch.*"*

*A man tries out for a job as a cantor. When he comes home
from the service, his wife asks him how it went.*

"Terrible. The shammes *said my voice was monotonous:
nobody liked the way I sang."*

*"Ah, what do you pay attention to him for?" the wife says.
"Everybody knows the* shammes *just repeats what he hears!"*

The synagogue too comes in for its share of ridicule:

*An elegantly dressed man starts up the steps of a large temple
on Yom Kippur. At the front door, a security guard stops him:
"Are you a member of this synagogue, sir?" the guard asks.*

"No."

*"Did you purchase a ticket to attend Rosh ha-Shana and
Yom Kippur services here?"*

"No, I did not," the man says.

*"I'm sorry," the guard says, "but you are forbidden to enter
the synagogue then."*

*The man is desperate. "I have a very important message to
give to Mr. Brian Goldstein. It's a matter of the greatest importance, an emergency. You must let me in to speak with him."*

*"Okay, okay," the guard finally says. "I'll let you in. But if
I catch you praying . . ."*

An aspect of Jewish communal life that is generally unknown (and, when known, unadmired) by non-Jews is that most
synagogues restrict attendance on the High Holy Days (Rosh ha-
Shana and Yom Kippur) to members or to nonmembers who
buy tickets in advance. Ticket prices for nonmembers are intentionally high, often in the hundreds of dollars, the goal being
to encourage them to join the synagogue. In practice, most synagogues will not actually turn away a person who tries to enter
without a ticket, but he or she might be asked to take a place
in the back of the sanctuary or to stand. Some large synagogues

Rabbi Joseph Telushkin

hire security guards, or ask prominent members, to check the tickets of all people coming in.*

Needless to say, this policy provokes quite a few furious complaints. Some angry people once complained to my grandfather, Rabbi Nissen Telushkin, who was the rabbi of a mid-sized, decidedly nonaffluent synagogue in Brooklyn. "It's disgusting," they said, "to ask people to buy tickets as if they were going to a movie or a sports event. Should a person be required to pay money before he can pray in a synagogue?"

"If a person doesn't have money, he or she shouldn't have to pay," my grandfather conceded. "But almost all the people who want to get in without tickets can afford to buy them. They just don't want to. They want the people who attend the synagogue year round to bear all the synagogue's expenses so that the synagogue will be available to them on the three days a year they deign to come. Doesn't it seem more just that they too should share in the expense of maintaining the synagogue?"

Incidentally, while it is common in Jewish life to censure Jews who only attend services on the High Holy Days ("Three-day-a-year Jews," they are sometimes called), there are tales in Jewish folklore extolling such people.

One Yom Kippur, an illiterate shepherd boy entered the synagogue where Israel Ba'al Shem Tov, the eighteenth-century founder of Hasidism, was praying. The boy was deeply moved by the service, but frustrated that he could not read the prayers. He started to whistle, the one thing he knew he could do beau-

---

*On very rare occasions, guards or ushers will rudely refuse would-be worshipers entrance to the synagogue. In *Still Talking,* comedian Joan Rivers writes that she bought tickets for High Holy Day services at a large temple in Manhattan. But when she arrived ten minutes late for the memorial service for the dead—her husband had died a few weeks earlier—the usher told her and her daughter that their seats had been given to others. Although the synagogue was not full, the usher, who was a prominent member of the congregation, refused to let them enter and pray. She was stunned, and furious: "I thought, This is temple? This is God?" (Joan Rivers with Richard Meryman, *Still Talking* [New York: Turtle Bay Books, Random House, 1991], p. 260).

tifully, as an offering to God. The congregation was horrified at the desecration of their service. Some people yelled at the boy, and others wanted to throw him out. The Ba'al Shem Tov immediately stopped them. "Until now," he said, "I could feel our prayers being blocked as they tried to reach the heavenly court. The young shepherd's whistling was so pure, however, that it broke through the blockage and brought all our prayers straight up to God."[12]

Jokes Rabbis Tell About Their Congregants

"If I had three more like you," a rabbi tells one of his opponents on the synagogue's board of directors, "I would be a happy man."

"What are you talking about, Rabbi?" the man responds. "I always criticize you. Why would you be happy if you had three more like me?"

"Because I have thirty more like you. If I had only three, I would be happy."

In the 1950s, Rabbi Max Arzt rose to make an announcement at the annual convention of the Rabbinical Assembly, the association of Conservative rabbis: "All rabbis who are happy with their board of directors will be meeting in a half hour on the second floor, in the telephone booth."

As suggested by the preceding two jokes, bullying by their boards is particularly irksome to rabbis:

A Jewish man, a stranger to the congregation, appears in the receiving line of a large synagogue with a famous rabbi. The stranger is accompanied by his ten-year-old son. "Rabbi, my young son here is thinking of becoming a rabbi. . . . Since you are our role model, we drove a hundred miles for him to meet you."

The rabbi glows, puts his hands on the boy's head, and says warmly: "Son, I'm delighted you're considering the rabbinate; a sacred calling. Now that you are here, coming such a great dis-

tance to meet me, is there a question you would like to put to me?"

"Yes," the kid says. "When you are not up there making speeches, what else do you do?"

The rabbi removes his hands, grimaces ever so slightly, and says: "Look, kid, you don't want to be a rabbi. You want to be a temple president."*

Perhaps the greatest frustration of all for rabbis is the indifference many lay leaders have toward Judaism's most fundamental values.

A rabbi is brought to speak before a congregation that is seeking a new spiritual leader.

"What will you be talking about?" the president asks the rabbi as they walk to the synagogue.

"Sabbath observance, the need for Jews to make this day truly holy, without shopping, without spending money."

"I wouldn't do that," the president warns. "The people here have very little free time; they must go shopping when they have the chance. Isn't there something else you think you could speak about?"

"Kashrut [Jewish dietary laws]."

"I wouldn't get into that, Rabbi. Don't you realize how difficult keeping kosher is out here? Kosher meat is much more expensive. Then the poor housewife has to keep two sets of dishes and silverware, and constantly worry that they don't get mixed up. Can't you speak about something else?"

"Okay, I'll speak about Jewish education, the need for day schools—"

"Are you crazy, Rabbi? The people here don't want to segregate Jews from everybody else. Besides, day-school hours are so long, it won't leave the kids any time for music lessons, dance classes, karate, basketball."

"I don't understand," the rabbi says. "If I can't speak about the Sabbath, about kashrut, *about Jewish education, what do you want me to speak about?"*

"Why, speak about Judaism of course."

---

*Albert Vorspan, *Start Worrying: Details to Follow*, pp. 39–40. Rabbis, whose days are spent going to committee meetings, counseling troubled congregants, visiting sick members in hospitals, teaching adult education and confirmation classes, are driven to distraction by the widespread perception that their sole obligation is to give a twenty-minute sermon at Sabbath services.

Orthodox Jewish Humor

Most Orthodox Jews in the United States speak a highly specialized vocabulary, in which Yiddish and Hebrew words mingle freely with English. While a Reform Jew might ask a friend, "Will you be going to temple Friday night?" an Orthodox Jew is more likely to ask: "What *shul* are you *davenning* [praying] in on *Shabbos*?"

Because Orthodox Jewish life incorporates numerous rituals and a vastly expanded "Jewish" vocabulary, its jokes generally are unintelligible to nontraditional Jews.

There is a surprisingly rebellious quality to much Orthodox humor; often, Jewish rituals are the target. For example, the Torah strictly forbids Jews from eating or possessing any leavened products, known in Hebrew as *khametz,* during Passover. On the morning before the holiday begins, religious Jews burn such *khametz* as bread, and they recite a prayer disavowing ownership of foodstuffs they may have inadvertently not destroyed.

More expensive *khametz,* such as whiskey and the utensils used to serve them, are hidden in the basement or a closed pantry for the holiday's duration. Since Torah law forbids Jews from even owning *khametz* during Passover, a rabbi, acting on behalf of the community, sells these products to a gentile, who makes a symbolic down payment and agrees not to take possession until after the holiday. As soon as Passover ends, the non-Jew tells the rabbi that he has decided not to put up the balance of the money. The sale is then immediately voided, and the *khametz* reverts to the possession of its Jewish owners. Thus, the Torah's demand that Jews not own *khametz* during Passover is fulfilled; at the same time, Jews do not have to destroy or sell valuable *khametz* at ridiculously low prices. All this is by way of background for the following story:

A number of years ago, Tel Aviv's Chief Rabbi, David Halevi, ruled that it was forbidden for Jews to smoke, on the grounds that smoking endangers health, and thus violates the biblical verse "Take heed to yourself and take care of your life" (Deuteronomy 4:9).

How did the rabbis of the various American-Jewish denominations react to Rabbi Halevi's ruling?

The Reform rabbis met and declared: "We are not bound by Jewish law [halakha], so Reform Jews can continue smoking if they please."

The Conservative rabbis met and decided: "Rabbi Halevi's ruling is a valid one. From now on, it is forbidden for Conservative rabbis to smoke." (Since everyone knows that the Conservative rabbis' rulings apply only to themselves, Conservative lay people rarely pay attention to them.)

The Orthodox rabbis met and declared: "Rabbi Halevi's ruling is a binding one. From now on, Orthodox Jews who smoke must first sell their lungs to goyim."

The joke is intentionally offensive to all Jews, for in addition to mocking the Orthodox ritual of selling *khametz,* it presents the characteristic Orthodox critique of non-Orthodox denominations: Reform rabbis don't care what the Torah or Jewish law says about anything; it doesn't apply to them. At an interdenominational dialogue in which I participated some years ago, shortly after the Reform movement had endorsed Cesar Chavez's boycott of grapes picked by underpaid Chicano laborers, a Conservative rabbi infuriated his Reform counterpart by observing: "A Reform rabbi who publicly eats pork on Yom Kippur will not get into trouble with the Central Conference of American Rabbis [the Reform rabbinical association] unless he has grapes for dessert."

The Conservative movement also comes in for its share of ridicule. Conservative Judaism claims that it is as committed to Jewish law as Orthodoxy, but that it is more open than the Orthodox to changing or modifying the law in accordance with historical circumstances. The claim, however, is truer in theory than practice. In real life, Jews who affiliate with Conservative synagogues tend to be quite unobservant of the Jewish rituals that their rabbis follow. As an Orthodox rabbi who became the spiritual leader of a Conservative synagogue once put it: "I'm an Orthodox rabbi in a Conservative synagogue with Reform members."

But the heart of the joke is a direct assault on a widely known Orthodox legal fiction. All religious systems based on divinely revealed texts seem to need such legal fictions (the Catholic Church sometimes grants marital annulments even to couples who have been together for years, as a way of evading the Church's ban on divorce). Without such "necessary fictions," religions would have to adhere literally to texts that could lead to grave financial losses, as in the case with *khametz,* or to terrible inequities, such as the inability of unhappily married Catholic couples to divorce.*

Much Orthodox humor attacks the extreme ritual punctiliousness of some observant Jews. One of the divisive issues in Jewish life is *kashrut.* In theory, a Jew who keeps kosher should be able to eat at the home of any other Jew who also keeps kosher. In practice, however, many Orthodox Jews will eat only in their own homes, at the homes of a few select people who are well known to them, or at restaurants under rabbinical supervision. Many are particularly careful about where they eat meat, since the laws regarding kosher slaughter are very complicated:

*Jewish law also has a legal fiction regarding the laws of divorce. Basing their ruling on a verse in the Torah (Deuteronomy 24:1), the rabbis concluded that only a man could grant a divorce, and he must do so willingly. Maimonides states, however, that if a Jewish court orders a man to grant a divorce and he refuses, he should be whipped until he says he wants to grant the divorce. Maimonides's rationale for why an agreement elicited through physical torture should be regarded as noncoercive sounds jocular. He reasons that since this man should give his wife a divorce—a Jewish court has urged him to do so—he is sinning, and must be doing so because a spirit of folly has possessed him. Therefore, by whipping him, we are in effect knocking out the spirit of folly and enabling him to do what his inner soul knows is right.

Jewish tradition promises that in the world-to-come, people will be served one of two foods: shor ha-bor *(wild ox) and Leviathan (a huge fish).*

A question is raised: Why isn't it sufficient to serve the wild ox? Why does God also need to provide fish on the menu?

Answer: For the sake of the very pious Jews who will say: "I am not sure about His kashrut. *Just let me have a piece of fish."*

Another topic for satire among the Orthodox is the talking that goes on during synagogue services. The Sabbath morning prayer service is long; in many congregations, it lasts for three hours or more. Most Orthodox Jews would not think of skipping this *davenning,* but when they become bored, they talk. The problem is a long-standing one in Jewish life; there are warnings against speaking during prayers in the medieval codes of Jewish law. Still, one Orthodox synagogue in Brooklyn mailed out the following questionnaire to its members:

Please check off your own areas of interest so that we can seat you during services with people who have shared interests. Do you prefer to sit near people who
• *talk about the stock market?*
• *share neighborhood gossip?*
• *sit quietly and actually pray?*
• *talk about sports?*

One reason the service is so long is because many prayers are repeated. The most important, the *Shmoneh Esray,* is first recited silently by the congregation, then chanted aloud by the cantor. Another prayer, *Yekum Purkan* ("May salvation arise"), is recited in Aramaic, a language that few modern Jews understand. It consists of two paragraphs that are remarkably similar to each other, each beginning with the words *Yekum Purkan.* Inevitably, this had to lead to a joke.

A minister, a priest, and a rabbi meet. They decide that because of the terrible problems of hatred and disunity in the world, they must formulate one religion to which all people can belong.

"In that case," the priest says, "we Catholics would be willing to give up belief in the Virgin Birth."

The minister and the rabbi are very impressed.

"In that case," the minister says, "we would be willing to give up the belief that faith in Christ atones for the sins of mankind."

The rabbi and priest are very impressed.

"In that case," the rabbi says, "we would be willing to give up the second Yekum Purkan."

While all Jews are familiar with the solemn fast of Yom Kippur, many are unaware of the six other fast days in the Jewish calendar, including one just before Purim, and another for firstborn sons just before Passover. Three other fast days recall the destruction of the two Temples.

The sixth fast day is observed on the third of Tishrei, the day after Rosh ha-Shana, and is known as *Tzom Gedaliah* (the Fast of Gedaliah). After the Babylonians defeated the Jewish kingdom of Judea in 586 B.C.E., they appointed Gedaliah, a Jew, to administer the province. The prophet Jeremiah, one of Gedaliah's major supporters, told the Jews to cooperate with him. But others viewed Gedaliah as a collaborator, and one fall day (circa 585 B.C.E.) they murdered him. After that, the Babylonians ruled Judea directly and brutally. Ever since, traditional Jews have observed the anniversary of Gedaliah's death as a fast day. Many Jews, however, have not exactly been stringent in this observance.

"Do you fast on Tzom Gedaliah?" *a Jew asks his friend.*

"No," the man answers.

"Why not?"

"I have not one reason, but three. First, if Gedaliah had not died when he did, he would be long dead by now anyway. Second, if I had died first, Gedaliah would not have fasted for me. And third, if I don't fast on Yom Kippur, why should I fast on Tzom Gedaliah?"

Orthodox jokes generally utilize Hebrew or Aramaic words, and presuppose a detailed knowledge of Jewish law. Reform or Conservative Jews would rarely joke about so specific a ritual as the *Tzom Gedaliah* fast because almost no non-Orthodox Jews observe it, and relatively few even know it exists.

I know of virtually no jokes about Jewish law among Reform Jews. One of the few Conservative jokes was recently told by William Novak in *Masoret,* the publication of the Conservative movement's Jewish Theological Seminary:

Bernie and Bernice, who belong to a Conservative congregation, maintain a kosher home. But like many of their fellow congregants, they will occasionally order more exotic fare in restaurants. Last summer, in fact, Bernie took his wife to Paris—just to eat. On the final night of their vacation, they go out for a sumptuous dinner at that most forbidden and alluring of all Parisian eateries, the venerable Chez Treif. *Knowing that this opportunity may never come again, Bernie decides to order the most expensive and outrageous item on the entire menu. An hour and a half later, four waiters walk in carrying Bernie's meal: an entire roast suckling pig, complete with all the trimmings—right down to the fruit in its mouth.*

No sooner does Bernie's meal arrive than who should walk into the restaurant but Bernie's hometown rabbi (presumably, there were some items on the menu that were not unkosher). As the rabbi comes over to say hello, Bernie jumps to his feet and does some fast thinking:

"Hello, Rabbi," he says. "I'm delighted to see you. You wouldn't believe *how fancy this place is. Why, just look at how they* potchkee *up a baked apple!"*

Even on the rare occasions when Orthodox jokes acknowledge flagrant violations of Jewish law, they are seldom so up front about it. A Jew who orders pork is not the sort of person who inhabits Orthodox jokes or the Orthodox world. But a Jew who ignores *Tzom Gedaliah* or who acknowledges violating some other, less serious ritual, *that* Jew is imaginable:

A Jew comes to a rabbi. "I committed a sin," he says, "and I want to know what I should do to make teshuva *[repent]."*

"What was the sin?" the rabbi asks.

"It happened once," the man answers, "that I didn't wash my hands and recite the blessing before eating bread."

"Nu, if it really only happened once," the rabbi says, "that's

*not so terrible. Nonetheless, why did you neglect to wash your
hands and recite the blessing?"*

*"I felt awkward, Rabbi, doing it. You see, I was in an unko-
sher restaurant."*

*The rabbi's eyebrows arch. "And why were you eating in an
unkosher restaurant?"*

"I had no choice. All the kosher restaurants were closed."

"And why were all the kosher restaurants closed?"

"It was Yom Kippur."

Charity

*At a circus, the strongman Hercules startles everyone with mag-
nificent feats of strength, lifting hundreds of pounds over his
head and putting a fist through a solid wall. For his final act,
he takes a lemon and squeezes it. At first, the juice dribbles out
quickly, then it slows down, and finally not a single drop comes
out. The circus manager steps forward and says: "I will personally give anyone who can squeeze even one more drop from
this lemon two hundred dollars." Two large men, both of whom
look like bouncers, step forward. Each one squeezes the lemon
with all his might, but not a drop comes out.*

"Does anyone else want to try?" the manager asks.

*A short, slightly built man steps forward. People in the
crowd snicker. The man picks up the lemon and squeezes it.
Juice gushes out. The manager is stunned. He steps forward with
two hundred-dollar bills, but when he hands them over, he can't
resist asking the man: "Who are you? What do you do?"*

*"Seymour Goldstein," the man answers. "I'm a fund-raiser
for the UJA [United Jewish Appeal]."*

Many of the most important themes in Jewish life and Jewish law are associated with charity, particularly the notion that
Jews are one extended family. For many years, the UJA's campaign slogan was "We are one." The American-Jewish community is organized through a network of charitable institutions.
Give to one Jewish charity, and within months you receive appeals from a dozen more.*

*"To disassociate effectively" from Jewish fund-raising appeals, argues Al-
bert Vorspan, "you have to enter an FBI Witness Relocation Program and
adopt a new identity" (Albert Vorspan, *Start Worrying: Details to Follow*, p.31).

The reason charity inspires jokes is because people are no-toriously reluctant to part with money, and Jewish charitable institutions are famous for influencing them to do precisely that. The Jewish community's level of charitable giving is much higher than that of American society as a whole. The best-known Jewish charity, the United Jewish Appeal—an organiza-tion whose potential constituency represents less than one in forty Americans—is among the United States's largest charities and collects more than a billion dollars annually.

This high level of giving results largely from the great em-phasis Judaism always has placed on charity. The Hebrew word *tzedaka* ("charity") is derived from *tzedek* (justice). The Tal-mud teaches, "*Tzedaka* is equal to all the other commandments combined" (*Bava Bathra* 9a).[13]

This perspective has made even *shnorrers* extremely self-confident, sometimes to the point of cockiness. In religious neighborhoods in Israel, beggars often assure donors that by giving them the opportunity to carry out a divinely ordained *mitzvah,* the recipient is doing the giver a favor.

A shnorrer is used to receiving a set donation from a certain man every week. One day, when he comes for the money, the man tells him that he can't give him anything: "I've had terrible expenses recently. My wife became very sick, and I had to send her to a health resort in Carlsbad. It's very cold there, so I had to buy her new clothes, and a fur coat."
"What!" the beggar yells. "With my money?"

Rabbi Jack Riemer, from whom I learned this story, claims that as far as Jewish law is concerned, "the beggar was right. In a very real sense it was *his* money, for the rich man and the poor man were both participants in a culture that was based on the premise that all property is ultimately God's, not man's, and that charity is a commandment, not a favor. Only among a peo-ple in whose language the same word means justice and charity could such a story be told."[14]

The Jews' legendary adeptness at fund-raising, however,

does not derive exclusively from their high-minded feelings of obligation. Equally important are the aggressive fund-raising techniques employed by Jewish institutions. Some local Jewish federations annually publish a booklet or other report listing the name of every donor and the amount of every significant contribution. Although many people claim to be offended by this document, they still read it avidly to see what their friends and enemies have given. Many large contributors acknowledge that if they received no communal recognition for their gifts, they would contribute less.[15] As the British-Jewish writer Chaim Bermant has written: "[The rabbis teach that] he who gives alms in secret is greater than Moses. [This] is not, by and large, the sort of greatness to which many Jews aspire."[16]

Unfortunately, the focus on *koved* (public honor) sometimes has its price:

An Israeli official, desperate to buy a new jet fighter that costs $50 million, comes up with an idea: He will seek out one thousand very wealthy Jews and ask them to give $50,000 each.

"But the plane wil never get off the ground," his friend tells him.

"Why not?"

"Do you have any idea how much a thousand plaques weigh?"

A very wealthy Jew has never contributed to the United Jewish Appeal. A delegation goes to solicit him.

"We've been checking up on you, Goldstein," the leader of the group tells the wealthy man. "We know everything. Not only do you own this house, which is a mansion, outright, we know about your place in Palm Springs and about the chalet in Switzerland. You drive a Rolls, your wife has a Mercedes, and we know you opened up twelve new stores this year."

Goldstein sits through the speech unperturbed; he doesn't flinch. "You think you checked so deeply into my background?" he says when the man finishes. "Well, did you also find out about my mother who's been in the hospital for three months with a very serious heart condition? Do you have any idea what round-the-clock nurses cost? Did you find out about my uncle who's in an asylum, and with no insurance? Did you check into my sister, who's married to a bum who can't keep a job, and who has two children in fancy colleges, and you know how much colleges cost today? . . . And if I don't give a penny to any of them, you think I'm going to give to you?"

The humor here lies in the fact that, as Isaac Asimov—who tells a version of this story in his *Treasury of Humor*—explains: "A rich Jew who would hesitate to give to charity could be accepted, but a rich Jew (or even a poor one) who failed to contribute to the support of his family, and even of a sick mother, is unthinkable."[17] Asimov tells another variation of the same story:

The rich Mr. Goldberg was brooding one day. Finally, he muttered to himself: "What good are my steamship lines to me; my oil stock; my department-store chain; all my hundreds of millions of dollars—when my poor mother is starving in an attic?"[18]

Much Jewish folklore also focuses on charity, particularly on the ingenious and witty ways Jewish fund-raisers have of convincing people to part with far more money than they ever intended.

Rabbi Joseph Kahaneman was the founder of the ultra-Orthodox, world-renowned Ponevitz yeshiva in B'nai B'rak, a suburb of Tel Aviv. During his world travels, Kahaneman raised funds to establish many Jewish schools.

Upon arriving in one city, he heard about a phenomenally wealthy local Jew. Kahaneman told a friend that he intended to solicit him. "It's a waste of time," his friend told him. "The man is violently anti-Orthodox. The moment he sees your long beard and coat, he won't give you a penny."

Sure enough, when Kahaneman met with the man, he proved to be as hostile to Orthodoxy as his friend had predicted.

"But surely," Rabbi Kahaneman entreated, "you want to help Jewish youngsters get a good education?"

"I'll tell you what," the man said. "Since education matters so much to you, let me make you an offer. I will give you all the money you need to build a Jewish elementary school, on one condition. The students are forbidden to wear a head-

*covering at any time, even when they study Torah or make a
blessing before eating."*

*"And if I accept this condition," Kahaneman answered,
"you will personally donate all the money that's needed."*

*The man laughed. "That sort of Jewish school, I'll happily
build."*

Kahaneman extended a hand. "Agreed."

*A year later, the man was invited to come to the school's
opening. On top of the beautiful building, a large sign proclaimed: "The New B'nai B'rak School for Girls."**

In another story, set in the 1920s:

*Shmaryahu Levin, a quick-witted Zionist leader, accompanied
the great Hebrew poet Hayyim Nachman Bialik on a fund-
raising mission to the United States. Bialik wanted to publish
the classic works of Jewish literature in an elegant new edition, and wished to initiate the project with a volume of
Hebrew poems by the thirteenth-century poet and philosopher
Solomon ibn Gabirol, one of the great figures of Spanish
Jewry's Golden Age.*

*Bialik and Levin went to see a wealthy Jew in Cleveland,
and Bialik outlined his proposal. "Waste of time to publish a
Hebrew poet," the wealthy man said to Bialik. "The Jewish people need another book of Hebrew poems like I need a hole in
the head. I wouldn't waste my money on such a project."*

*"But the poor poet has died, and left behind a widow
with six young children," Levin broke in, neglecting to mention that ibn Gabirol's death had occurred some seven centuries earlier.*

*"Oh, in that case," the wealthy man said, taking out his
checkbook, "I'll give you five hundred dollars."*

As the story notes, many Jewish philanthropists have warm
Jewish hearts but relatively ignorant Jewish heads.

A nineteenth-century folktale is set in a small *shtetl* in
Russia, where a terrible cold wave was causing extreme suf-

*For those unacquainted with Jewish rituals, Jewish males of all ages must
cover their heads; unmarried women and girls do not.

fering to the poor. On one bitingly cold day, the rabbi went to solicit the only wealthy man in town, a man known to be a miser.

The rabbi knocked, and the man opened the door.

"Come in, Rabbi," the rich man said. Unlike everyone else in the town, he was only in shirtsleeves; after all, his house was well heated.

"No," the rabbi said. "No need for me to come in. I'll just be a minute."

The rabbi then proceeded to engage the rich man in a lengthy conversation, asking him detailed questions concerning each member of his family. The man was shivering, yet every time he asked the rabbi to come inside, the rabbi refused.

"And your wife's cousin, the lumber merchant, how is he?" the rabbi asked.

The rich man's cheeks were fiery red. "What did you come here for, Rabbi?"

"Oh, that," the rabbi said. "I need money from you to buy coal for the poor people in town."

"So why don't you come in and we'll talk about it?"

"Because if I come in, we will sit down by your fireplace. You will be very warm and comfortable and when I tell you how the poor are suffering from the cold, you really won't understand. You'll give me five rubles, maybe ten, and send me away. But now, out here," the rabbi went on, indicating the frozen moisture on the man's cheeks, "when I tell you how the poor are suffering from the cold, I think you'll understand better. Right?"

The man was happy to give the rabbi a hundred rubles, just so he could shut the door and return to his fireplace.

8

"Better to Be Late in This World Than Early in the Next" Why Are There So Few Funny Israeli Jokes?

▶

President Nixon asks Prime Minister Golda Meir to send General Moshe Dayan to the United States in return for any three generals she wants.

Golda agrees. "We'll give you General Dayan. You give us General Motors, General Electric, and General Telephone."

There is not a great deal of humor being created in Israel, and most of what exists is not very funny, at least not to non-Israelis. Because people in power are able to deal with their problems directly, they have no need to settle for the personal gratification of a sharp put-down or witticism. Israelis, for example, don't joke much about their Arab opponents; they fight them.

The jokes that do circulate about the extraordinarily successful Israeli Army, such as the previous one, are usually made up by American Jews and reflect American sensibilities:

During the Six-Day War an Israeli tank collides with an Egyptian tank in the Sinai desert.

> *The Egyptian jumps out of his tank yelling, "I surrender."*
> *The Israeli jumps out yelling, "Whiplash."*

And comedian David Berry tells this one:

Moshe Dayan promised to give back the Arab lands, only they're now in his wife's name.[1]

The funniest jokes created by Israelis deal with those aspects of life about which they feel powerless: the economy, the country's horrendous drivers, the bureaucracy that has resulted from decades of state socialism, the politicization of every aspect of life, the widespread rudeness of the population, and *yerida* (emigration from Israel).

The economy seems to inspire more jokes than any other subject, and with good reason: It is almost always in poor shape. In September 1983, for example, the exchange rate was 60 Israeli shekels to the dollar; two years later, the rate was 1,500. The surging inflation sparked a host of riddles:

Why is it cheaper to travel in Israel by bus than by taxi?
Because in the bus you have to pay at the beginning of the ride, in the taxi at the end.

What's the difference between a dollar and a shekel?
A dollar.

And an old perennial resurrected during every economic crisis:

How do you make a small fortune in Israel?
Come with a large one.

Such jokes exaggerate—but not by much. During the runaway inflation of the early 1980s, the official rate of exchange between the dollar and the shekel was revised twice daily, in the morning and again in the afternoon. This galloping inflation had many adverse effects on citizen morale. For example, in America, prompt payment of bills is regarded as virtuous; in

Israel, it was seen as stupid. Delay paying your phone bill for three weeks, and the inflation rate alone effectively made it 10 percent cheaper.

Israeli digs at their country's dire economic situation are as old as the state. Shortly after Israel's creation in 1948, the following story circulated:

Prime Minister David Ben-Gurion offered a friend a cabinet position, minister of colonies.

"But we have no colonies," the friend protested.

"So what?" Ben-Gurion said. "Kaplan is minister of finance."

This joke tends to be adapted to different societies. In a version circulated by Russian dissidents during the 1970s, Foreign Minister Andrei Gromyko visits Luxembourg. The entire cabinet is presented to him, and when he meets the minister of defense, Gromyko starts laughing: "Your country is so small, you have nothing to defend."

"That's no reason for you to laugh," the minister says: "Last year in Moscow I met your minister of justice."

Since Israel's establishment in 1948, its largely socialist-inspired bureaucracy has kept growing. Americans who move to the Jewish state find themselves wasting a significant percentage of their waking hours obtaining items that could be acquired in the United States almost immediately—for example, telephone service:

An American moved to Israel and immediately applied to have a telephone installed. Three weeks later, he still had not heard from the phone company, so he returned to its office. He was sent to a high official in the company. "When did you apply for the phone?" the official asked.

The American gave the precise date.

"But that's only a few weeks ago." The official picked up a stack of much older applications, which had still not been filled. "There are so many people ahead of you."

> *"Does that mean I have no hope?"*
> *The Israeli looked up sternly. "It is forbidden for a Jew ever to say, 'I have no hope.' No chance, maybe."*

Indeed, the name of the Israeli national anthem is *Ha-Tikvah,* which means "The Hope."

Another source of jokes is the Israeli character:

> *An American, a Pole, a Chinaman, and an Israeli are standing on a street corner when a man comes over with a clipboard.*
> *"Excuse me," he says, "I am taking a poll. What is your opinion of the meat shortage?"*
> *The American asks: "What's a 'shortage'?"*
> *The Pole asks: "What's 'meat'?"*
> *The Chinaman asks: "What's an 'opinion'?"*
> *The Israeli asks: "What's 'excuse me'?"*

Israelis do not commonly think of their society as rude but as *dugri,* Hebrew slang that suggests no beating around the bush. Over the years, several Israelis have told me that they think Americans are rude. "They'll invite you to visit them," one Israeli complained, "but as soon as you try to pin them down to a date, it becomes apparent that the invitation was not sincerely intended." Israel is in fact the most hospitable society with which I'm familiar.

On the other hand, virtually every tourist to Israel comes back with at least one story about Israeli aggressiveness. A friend of mine, who is six feet four, was first in a crowded line waiting for a bus. "The bus finally came," he recalled. "Only when it pulled out, everybody who was in back of me had gotten on. I was still on the curb. Even short grandmothers with sharp elbows had pushed in front of me, until there was no room left." The story sounds unbelievable only to those who have never visited Israel.

Sadly, this aggressiveness finds expression on the highways. The homicidal driving of many of its citizens generally inspires more anguish than humor in Israel. As many people have died in road accidents as were killed in Israel's five wars with the Arabs. In Israel, accidents are overwhelmingly caused by speeding, tailgating, and other types of recklessness, unlike in the United States, where about two thirds of traffic fatalities are a result of drunk driving. There are two aphorisms about driving in Israel:

"Better to be late than 'the late.'"

"Better to be late in this world than early in the next."

Anyone who has ridden a bus in Israel can appreciate the following:

An Israeli bus driver and a pious rabbi die on the same day. They are brought before the heavenly tribunal, and the bus driver is immediately admitted to heaven. The rabbi is told to wait; his case must be examined more carefully.

The rabbi is outraged: "I know for a fact that that bus driver was a totally irreligious Jew, while I gave a shiur *in Talmud every day."*

"That is all very true," the heavenly angel tells him. "But when you taught Talmud you caused many people to sleep. When that driver drove his bus, everybody prayed."

Israel is an extraordinarily politicized society. In an average election campaign, 20 or more parties compete for seats in the 120-member Knesset (parliament). Once elected, members often heckle each other far more viciously than do their counterparts in the U.S. House of Representatives or Senate. During one stormy debate in 1991, an Orthodox parliamentarian, Rabbi Menachem Porush, accused an M.K. (member of the Knesset) from a secular party of advocating Nazi-like attitudes toward Judaism. While many reacted by lamenting the decline of civility in Israeli politics, others noted that Porush's attack was "par for the course." In 1963, Prime Minister David Ben-Gurion charged that if Knesset member (and future prime minister) Menachem Begin gained power, "he will . . . rule the way Hitler ruled Germany. . . . I have no doubt that Begin hates Hitler, but that hatred does not prove that he is unlike [Hitler]."[2]

Ben-Gurion's imputation of totalitarianism to Begin aside, during 1948–1977, when Ben-Gurion's Labor party ruled Israel, adherents of opposition parties often found it hard to obtain work:

In the early 1950s, an American Jew makes aliyah [emigrates] to Israel. He goes to a government employment office in Tel Aviv.
  "What did you do in America?" he is asked.
  "I was an economist."
  "Excellent. We need economists. Go to room twenty."
  In room 20 he is asked: "What academic degrees do you have?"
  "An M.A. from the London School of Economics, and a Ph.D. from Harvard."
  "Very good. Go to room thirty."
  There he is asked: "Have you ever worked in pensions?"
  "Yes. As a matter of fact that was my specialty at the U.S. Department of Labor."
  "Wonderful. Go to room forty."
  In room 40 he is asked: "What political party do you belong to?"
  "I'm not a member of any party."
  "Please go through Door A over there," he is instructed. The American walks through the door and finds himself out on the sidewalk.

Politics was not the only challenge facing Israeli workers. In Europe, there were few Jewish farmers. Jews were generally forbidden to own land, and so were disproportionately drawn to urban living. Zionism revolutionized Jewish life by insisting that Jews would only be able to run their own state when they performed the kinds of physical tasks—farming and construction—that they had rarely performed in the Diaspora. The Zionist vision captured the Jewish imagination: In Palestine during the 1920s and 1930s, farmers had more status than teachers and other professionals.

However, when the 1967 war ended, Israel suddenly found itself with well over a million Arab residents: Within a few years, Arabs were doing most of the physical labor, as the following joke suggests:

A young Israeli boy is walking with his grandfather. They pass a large tree and the grandfather says, "When I was a young man I planted that tree." Later, they pass a beautiful old house. "When I was a young man," the grandfather says, "I built that house."

The young boy looks at the old man. "When you were young, Grandfather, were you an Arab?"

Throughout the 1970s and 1980s, Israeli Jews' occupational patterns increasingly came to resemble those of their co-religionists in the West. Like their American-Jewish counterparts, Israeli parents long to speak of "my son the doctor," not "my son the kibbutznik."

Jews' relations with their Arab neighbors have been complicated, to say the least. As Rabbi Irving Greenberg acerbically quipped:

If we Jews are five percent better than the rest of the world, we can be a "light unto the nations." If we are twenty-five percent better than the rest of the world, we can bring the Messiah. If we're fifty percent better than the rest of the world, we'll all be dead.

With considerable justification, Israelis feel that the world holds them to a standard to which it holds no other country. During periods when Arab states have murdered tens of thousands of their own citizens—in 1982, the Syrians killed up to twenty thousand people in Hama,[3] while during the Iran-Iraq war, the Iraqis murdered thousands of Kurds with poison gas—Israel was denounced as racist and criminal whenever rock-throwing Palestinians were killed in clashes with Israeli troops. "After two years of Arab terror," Israeli Prime Minister Golda Meir said in 1969, "there has not been one execution in Israel. Instead of executing terrorists, we destroy houses which shelter them. So knocking down a house becomes a barbaric act."*

The widespread international prejudice against Israel was most sharply expressed in the United Nations General Assembly's 1975 resolution condemning Zionism as racism. Zionism, the national liberation movement of the Jews, was the only such national movement so condemned. (In late 1991, the "Zionism is racism" resolution was repealed.)

In the eyes of the U.N., Israel can do no right. During the late 1970s and early 1980s, Iraqi President Saddam Hussein often boasted that he was going to build an atom bomb and destroy Israel. In 1981, Israeli pilots bombed and destroyed Hussein's nuclear reactor in Osirak with virtually no loss of Iraqi lives. The reaction? Universal condemnation of Israel.

Abba Eban, Israel's longtime foreign minister and ambassador to the U.N., claimed that if an Arab nation introduced a motion that the world was flat and that it had been flattened by Israeli tanks, it would pass the General Assembly by a resounding majority. No wonder that when the Soviet Union invaded Czechoslovakia in 1968, Israeli humorist Ephraim Kishon predicted that a U.N. resolution would be passed condemning Israel for the Soviet invasion.

In recent years, the following story circulated in Israel:

An American, an Englishman, and an Israeli are captured by cannibals. They are each permitted one last wish before being thrown into an enormous boiling pot.

---

*Golda Meir's well-honed common sense, anger, and wit were not only directed against Israel's opponents. During the early years of the state, several rapes were reported to have been committed. At a cabinet meeting, one member proposed that women not be allowed to go out alone at night until the rapists were caught.

"I don't understand the proposal," Golda Meir, the only woman in the cabinet, declared. "It's men who are committing the rapes. Men should not be allowed out at night."

The American takes off his wedding ring, and gives it to the cannibal chief. "Please have this sent back to my wife."

The Englishman asks permission to sing "God Save the Queen."

The Israeli says to the chief: "I want you to give me a very hard kick in the ass."

The chief complies and sends the Israeli sprawling, but when he gets up, he whips out a gun and shoots the chief dead, then starts firing at the other cannibals until they all flee.

The American and the Englishman are very grateful but puzzled. "Why did you tell him to kick you in the ass first? Why didn't you just take out the gun right away?"

"Oh, that I couldn't do," the Israeli says. "I didn't want to be denounced as the aggressor."

This extraordinarily bitter joke is based in no small measure on Israel's experience during the 1973 Yom Kippur War. Hours before the war erupted, Israeli Chief of Staff David Elazar warned Prime Minister Golda Meir that an attack from Egypt and Syria was imminent, and requested permission to launch a preemptive air strike, such as that which had led Israel to victory in the 1967 war. Meir forbade Elazar to launch an offensive, for if Israel attacked first, whatever the provocation, she would be denounced as the aggressor and the United States might withhold the arms she needed to fight. The "kick in the ass" that Israel took during the Yom Kippur War was far worse than anything Golda had feared: 2,700 Israeli soldiers died during the ensuing weeks. "I shall live with that terrible knowledge for the rest of my life," she wrote in her autobiography.[4]

Zionism's goal was to establish a homeland to which Jews from around the world would emigrate. It has been a bitter disappointment, therefore, that the waves of immigration that have built up the country have been made up almost entirely of Jews without alternatives: German Jews during the 1930s; Holocaust survivors in 1948–49; Jews from the Arab world during the late 1940s and 1950s; Ethiopian Jews, starting in the 1980s;

and Russian Jews in the 1970s, and again in the late 1980s and early 1990s.

Even more frustrating to Israelis is the high rate of emigration; during a typical year, five or six times as many Israeli Jews migrate to the United States as do American Jews to Israel. People who move from Israel are called *yordim* (from the Hebrew word *yored,* which means "to descend"). Since Israel's establishment in 1948, an estimated 500,000 Israelis have become *yordim* to the United States.

Perhaps because of lingering guilt feelings about leaving a besieged country, almost all former Israelis insist that they will return to their homeland someday—after they make enough money. No one has yet figured out how much money is enough, and in general few *yordim* return to Israel.

The several hundred thousand Israelis living in America petition the President to grant them their own small country. The request is granted, the country is established, only they can't find anyone willing to serve as ambassador to Israel.

In Israeli humor, people who leave Israel for other countries are frequently stigmatized as being without scruples:

An Israeli man visits a brothel in an isolated town in the American Midwest and informs the madam that he is prepared to pay $100, but only for an Israeli woman. "That's an amazing coincidence," says the delighted proprietor, "because we happen to have one right here." The man is taken to her chamber, where they silently make love. When they are finished, the customer thanks the prostitute in Hebrew.

"Don't tell me you're an Israeli, too?" says the lady.

"Yes, I'm from Haifa."

"That's wonderful," says the prostitute. "I'm from Haifa also. My brother still lives there. Maybe you know him—Chaim Cohen?"

"I do know him," says the man. "I know him very well. As a matter of fact, he gave me a hundred dollars to give to you."[5]

*   *   *

Many Western Jews will do anything for Israel, except live there. As the late British rabbi Kopul Rosen once said: "That all Jews nowadays are Zionists goes without saying, but that all Zionists should live in Israel is said without going."

Several thousand young American Jews volunteered to work in Israel during the Six-Day War. At a reception with Golda Meir before returning to the United States, she challenged them: "You were ready to die with us. Why don't you live with us?" In fact, from those countries in which Jews have equal rights, only a very small percentage have emigrated to Israel. It is rare for more than two to three thousand of America's five and a half million Jews to make *aliyah* in any one year. There are many pious Jews who live their whole lives in the Diaspora, then leave instructions to have their bodies rushed to Israel for burial. It is this group—along with know-it-all Israeli officials—that are the target in this final joke:

A woman arrives at El Al in New York to board a plane for Israel. She is carrying a dog inside a small carrying case.

"I want to take the dog with me on the flight," she tells the chief steward.

"That's not permitted," he says.

"I want the dog with me," she yells.

The steward assures her that the airline will keep the dog carrier in a designated part of the luggage section, and that the dog will be totally safe. If, however, she continues to insist that the dog be seated alongside her, neither she nor the dog will be permitted to board. The woman finally relents, and the dog is taken away.

When the plane arrives at Ben Gurion Airport, the steward sees to his horror that the dog is dead. He is in dread; what will he tell the woman? He summons an assistant: "Look," he says, "this dog is a light brown cocker spaniel. Just rush right down to Tel Aviv, buy a light brown cocker spaniel the size of this one, and come right back. She won't know the difference."

The steward stalls the woman, telling her that customs officials must make numerous inspections before approving the dog's entry into the country.

Finally, the assistant arrives with the dog. The steward removes the dead dog from the carrier, substitutes the new one, and goes out to the woman.

She takes one look at the dog and starts screaming. "This isn't my dog! This isn't my dog!"

"Of course it's your dog, madam," the steward says.

"It's not, it's not!" she says.

"How do you know?"

"Because my dog is dead. I was bringing him to be buried in the Holy Land."

9

"Why is This Knight Different from All Other Knights?" Seven Final—and Unrelated—Jewish Jokes

▶

It's 3:00 A.M. and a woman wakes up to see her husband pacing the floor. "Why can't you sleep?" she asks him.

"You know our next door neighbor, Sam. I borrowed a thousand dollars from him, and it's due tomorrow morning, and I don't have the money. I don't know what I'm going to do." The woman gets out of bed and opens the window. "Sam!" she shouts, and several times more, "Sam, Sam!"

Finally a very groggy man opens the window opposite her: "Wha . . . What is it?"

"You know the thousand dollars my husband owes you? He doesn't have it."

She slams the window shut. "Now," she says to her husband, "you go to sleep and let him pace the floor."

This joke, I have often noted, particularly appeals to the clergy (and, I suspect, to psychiatrists and others in the helping professions). It reminds me of the story about a woman who goes to speak with her rabbi. For more than two hours, she unburdens herself, telling him in detail about her husband's inoperable brain tumor, her married son with two small children who has just been fired from his job, and her terrible financial problems. Suddenly she smiles at the rabbi. "It's amazing," she says. "When I came here, I had a terrible headache, but now it's disappeared."

"You're mistaken, madam," the rabbi says. "The headache hasn't disappeared. I have it now."

A Jewish woman goes into labor, and her husband takes her to the hospital. Throughout the night, he hears moans coming from her room. He's a nervous wreck, pacing back and forth hour after hour, sweat running down his face.

Finally, the doctor rushes out. "Congratulations! You have a girl."

"Thank God," the man says. "She'll never have to go through what I just did."

What mattered to this man was his anxiety, not his wife's pain. This joke brings to mind the words of the late Rabbi Wolfe Kelman: "Always remember! What's central to you is peripheral to other people."

Paskudnyak, a Russian word incorporated into Yiddish, describes an odious character, a good-for-nothing bum. In *Hurray for Yiddish!*, Leo Rosten defines *paskudnyak* through a story about a landlord:

Mr. Elfenbein said to Rabbi Hyman: "It's too sad to believe! Imagine, Rabbi, a widow, three little children, owes four hundred dollars in rent and unless she pays before Friday, she'll be evicted."

"How terrible," said the rabbi. "I'll make an appeal. And here is fifty dollars of my own money."

"Thank you, Rabbi."

"You are a good man, Mr. Elfenbein. Are you related to the widow?"

"Oh no."

> *"What got you interested in this case?"*
> *"I'm the landlord."*[1]

Although American Jews have long been upwardly mobile, many spent their first years in this country living in cramped apartments in tenement buildings. Actress Molly Picon, who started her career on the Yiddish stage, used to brag to friends that her mother raised ten children in four rooms.

"How did she manage?" someone asked.

"She took in boarders."

Given this context, it is no surprise that landlords became the targets of many other acerbic jokes:

A young Jewish woman, pursuing a graduate degree in art history, is going to Italy to study the country's greatest works of art. Since there is no one in New York to look after her grandmother, she takes the old lady along. At the Sistine Chapel in the Vatican, she points to the painting on the ceiling. "Grandma, it took Michelangelo a full four years to get that ceiling painted."

"Oh my God!" the grandmother says. "He and I must have the same landlord."

A Woody Allen monologue from the 1960s, when he worked as a stand-up comic, remains one of his most consummately Jewish creations:

"Here's a story you're not going to believe. I shot a moose once. I was hunting in upstate New York and I shot a moose.

"And I strap him onto the fender of my car, and I'm driving along the West Side Highway. But what I didn't realize was that the bullet did not penetrate the moose. It just creased his scalp, knocking him unconscious. And I'm driving through the Holland Tunnel and the moose wakes up.

"So I'm driving with a live moose on my fender and the moose is signaling for a turn. And there's a law in New York State against driving with a conscious moose on your fender, Tuesdays, Thursdays, and Saturdays. And I'm very panicky. And then it hits me—some friends of mine are having a costume party. I'll go. I'll take the moose. I'll ditch him at the party. It won't be my responsibility. So I drive up to the party and I knock on the door and the moose is next to me. My host comes to the door. I say, 'Hello, you

know the Solomons.' We enter. The moose mingles. Did very well. Scored. Some guy was trying to sell him insurance for an hour and a half.

"Twelve o'clock comes, they give out prizes for the best costume of the night. First prize goes to the Berkowitzes, a married couple dressed as a moose. The moose comes in second. The moose is furious. He and the Berkowitzes lock antlers in the living room. They knock each other unconscious. Now, I figure, here's my chance. I grab the moose, strap him on my fender, and shoot back to the woods. But I've got the Berkowitzes.

"So I'm driving along with two Jewish people on my fender. And there's a law in New York State. Tuesdays, Thursdays, and especially Saturday.

"The following morning, the Berkowitzes wake up in the woods in a moose suit. Mr. Berkowitz is shot, stuffed, and mounted at the New York Athletic Club. And the joke is on them, 'cause it's restricted."[2]

On first reading, the Jewish strain in this monologue seems conveyed solely by the name Berkowitz and the reference to the New York Athletic Club's antisemitism. Read this routine again, however, and it becomes apparent that every major element in it has a Jewish association, beginning with Woody Allen practicing the paradigmatically non-Jewish sport of hunting. Walter Rathenau, the Jewish foreign minister of the Weimar Republic during the early 1920s, and a man who often associated with the hunt-loving German aristocracy, observed that "when a Jew says he's going hunting to amuse himself, he lies."

Thousands of years ago, the laws of kosher slaughter ordained that any animal permitted to be eaten had to be killed instantaneously with one uninterrupted knife-stroke. This effectively made hunting off-limits to Jews, since any animal killed in a hunt was automatically forbidden as food.[3]

A psychological reason for the long-standing Jewish abhorrence of hunting was articulated by Heinrich Heine in 1826: "My ancestors did not belong to the hunters as much as to the hunted, and the idea of attacking . . . those who were our comrades in misery goes against my grain." Heine's point is acutely insightful. When a Jew sees an animal fleeing a hunter's rifle and trying to hide, with whom does the Jew identify—the man from the NRA or his target?*

What happens in the Woody Allen monologue?

He shoots an animal for sport, a morally problematic act. But he is saved from his cruel action because the animal is un-injured. So although the story starts off with an unfunny prem-ise, "I shot a moose once," we now feel free to laugh.

"I'll take the moose," Allen goes on to say. "I'll ditch him at the party. It won't be my responsibility."

Responsibility, like justice, is another typical Jewish obses-sion. One of Judaism's most important characteristics is its ob-session with responsibilities more than with rights. For example, while contemporary American culture places great emphasis on consumer rights, Jewish law stated two millennia ago that consumers also have obligations. "One is forbidden," the Talmud rules, "to ask the storekeeper the price of an item if one has no intention of buying it" (Mishna *Bava Mezia* 4:10). And while American society puts primary emphasis on the right of free speech, Jewish law places greater emphasis on the speaker's responsibilities of speech—not to pass on negative in-formation about a person unless the hearer absolutely needs this information.

Finally, the story's moral punch line: Two Jews get into the New York Athletic Club, which long tried to bar all Jews. Allen's ridiculing of antisemitism reminds us, probably intentionally, of Groucho Marx's sardonic telegram to a country club that had denied entrance to his son (see page 109).

An elderly Jewish man reads about an inexpensive cruise to Florida, only fifty dollars. He signs up. Immediately, he is thrown

---

*For all that Jews opposed hunting, traditional Jewish culture never had a love affair with animals. In Eastern Europe, dogs were associated with peas-ants, who sometimes set them upon Jews. An old Jewish folk saying claimed that an apostate retains two Jewish characteristics: He falls asleep Saturday afternoon after lunch, and he's afraid of dogs.

into the galley of a ship, tied to his seat, and forced to start rowing, along with a hundred other men. A vicious-looking man walks up and down the aisle, cracking a whip across the back of anyone not rowing fast enough. The old man is at the point of collapse when the ship, after two weeks at sea, finally pulls into Miami Beach. He turns to the man next to him, "I've never been on one of these cruises before. How much do we tip the whipper?"

Finally, a joke about Jewish guilt or, better yet, Jewish masochism. This poor, bruised Jew has only one concern when he finally makes it to Miami Beach, how to reward the man who is responsible for his suffering.

Then again, the joke might have less to do with Jewish guilt than with cowardice. Although the original intention of offering a tip was "to ensure promptness," and to reward particularly good service, tips today are also given for service that is indifferent or bad. As Will Rogers put it, "I wonder if it ain't just cowardice, instead of generosity, that makes us give most of our tips."

Perhaps because it is the most widely observed Jewish holiday, Passover inspires more jokes than any other (see, for example, pages 161–162). The holiday's central ceremony is the Seder, a ritual meal celebrated at home with family and friends. Participants read aloud from the *Haggadah,* a short book that tells the story of the Hebrews' Exodus from Egyptian slavery.

The *Haggadah*'s best-known passage begins, *"Ma nish-ta-na ha-laila ha-zeh mi-kol ha-lei-lot?"* ("Why is this night different from all other nights?"). It goes on to ask four questions concerning the rituals that distinguish the Passover meal from a normal one (e.g., "On all other nights we eat leavened and unleavened bread, on this night [why do we eat] only unleavened bread?").

The *Ma Nish-ta-na,* as Jews usually refer to it, is traditionally recited by the youngest participant at the Seder; Jewish children as young as three or four are taught how to chant the Four Questions. For most Jewish children, this recitation represents their first public speaking. Unfortunately, for more than a few Jewish adults, it also may well be the sum total of Hebrew they know. Thus, the following:

An English Jew, a prominent novelist and intellectual, is informed that he will be knighted. The queen's protocol officials prepare him and other knights-to-be for the ceremony. He is informed that, when he stands before the queen, he is to recite certain Latin words just before being knighted.

On the day of the ceremony, the man is very nervous and, sure enough, when he approaches the queen, he forgets the Latin expression. As precious seconds tick by, the only non-English words that he knows pour out of him: "Ma nish-ta-na ha-laila ha-zeh mi-kol ha-leilot?" *The queen, confused, turns to her protocol officer and asks:* "Why is this knight different from all other knights?"

Notes

▶

Introduction: What Is Jewish About Jewish Humor?

1. On the basis of a 1988 survey comparing American Jews and non-Jews, sociologist Steven M. Cohen estimated "... [that] per capita Jewish income may actually be double that of non-Jews." Cohen's study is cited in Seymour Martin Lipset, "A Unique People in an Exceptional Country," Seymour Martin Lipset, ed., *American Pluralism and the Jewish Community* (New Brunswick, N.J.: Transaction Publishers, 1990), p. 3. A 1975 study noted that Jewish earnings in the U.S. were some 72 percent above the national average (Thomas Sowell, *Ethnic America* [New York: Basic Books, 1981], p. 5).

2. To mention a glaring but hardly unique example: In a 1963 Knesset debate, Prime Minister David Ben-Gurion predicted that if Knesset member, and future prime minister, Menachem Begin gained political power, "he will replace the army ... and rule the way Hitler ruled Germany" (cited in Michael Bar-Zohar, *Ben-Gurion: A Biography* [New York: Delacorte Press, 1977], p. 303).

3. In the case of the two men coming into court and clutching the same garment, the Mishnah, the oldest section of the Talmud, rules as follows: "If this one says, 'It is all mine,' and the other one says, 'It is all mine,' then this one must swear that he does not own less than a half, and the other must swear that he does not own less than a half and they divide it [dividing means that each gets half of the value of the cloak]. If this one says, 'It is all mine,' and the other one says, 'It is half mine [because he believes they discovered it simultaneously]'—then the one who says, 'It is all mine' must swear that he does not own less than three quarters, and the one who says, 'Half of it is mine' must swear that he does not own less than a quarter, and this one takes three quarters and this one takes one quarter." The

reasoning behind this unusual oath is explained in Louis Jacobs, *Jewish Law* (New York: Behrman House, 1968), pp. 33–35.

4. See Salcia Landmann, "On Jewish Humor," *The Jewish Journal of Sociology,* 4:2, December 1962, p. 201. The reasoning process put forth by the adulterer in this joke is known in the Talmud as *kal va-khomer,* and is discussed further on pp. 53–55.

5. Christie Davies, "Jewish Jokes, Anti-Semitic Jokes and Hebredonian Jokes," in Avner Ziv, ed., *Jewish Humor,* p.78. (Full bibliographical references are not provided for books listed in the Bibliography.)

6. Jackie Mason, *Jackie Mason's 'The World According to Me!,'* p. 74.

7. Thomas Sowell, *Ethnic America, op. cit.,* p. 5.

8. Nathan Glazer and Daniel Patrick Moynihan, *Beyond the Melting Pot* (Cambridge, Mass.: M.I.T. Press, 1970), p. 257.

9. Having denounced the viciousness of this joke, I must acknowledge that there is a Jewish version, although it is told in a totally different context. According to Israeli psychologist and scholar of humor Avner Ziv, the following story circulated in Israel in the aftermath of the Yom Kippur War:

> *Two soldiers are sitting in a small, cramped bar. "You could easily fit an entire tank division in here," says one.*
> *"How?"*
> *"In an ashtray" (Avner Ziv,* Personality and Sense of Humor, *p. 54).*

Ziv notes, however, that such jokes were told by the tank corps and other Israeli soldiers, not by the general public. Any Israeli not in the army who told this joke would have risked being physically attacked, as would any Israeli or Jew who might direct it against Holocaust victims.

10. Lore and Maurice Cowan, *The Wit of the Jews,* p. 142. The greatest Yiddish writer, Sholom Aleichem, similarly combined irony and sarcasm in reporting a conversation between two children emigrating with their parents to America following a pogrom:

> *I ask him, what's a pogrom? I hear all the emigrants talking about "pogrom" but I have no idea what it is. Kopl gloats over me: "You don't know what a pogrom is? Gee, you are dumb! Pogroms are everywhere these days. They start from nothing, but once they start, they go on for three days."*

"But what is it," I ask, "a fair?"

"Some fair! They break windows, smash furniture, tear up pillows—feathers fly like snow."

"What for?"

"What for? For nothing! A pogrom isn't only against houses, it's against stores too. They smash all the stores, throw everything out into the streets or steal it, push things around, douse everything with kerosene, strike a match, and burn it up."

"Don't be funny."

"What do you mean, y'think I'm kidding? Then, when there's nothing left to steal, they go from house to house with axes and sticks, followed by the police. They sing and whistle and shout, 'Hey, guys, kill the dirty Jews!' They smash, kill, stab with spears. . . ."

"Who?"

"What do you mean who? Jews!"

"What for?"

"What for? Cause it's a pogrom!"

"So if it's a pogrom, so what?"

"Get away, you're an ass. I don't want to talk to you," Kopl says to me, pushes me away, and puts his hands in his pockets like a grownup" (cited in Meyer Wiener, "On Sholom Aleichem's Humor," in Sarah Blacher Cohen, ed., Jewish Wry: Essays on Jewish Humor, *p. 38).*

11. In the sixteen-volume *Encyclopedia Judaica,* there is an extraordinary entry about one Ignatius Timothy Trebitsch-Lincoln (1879–1943), a man who might well have been the model for the "Jew in Warsaw." At the age of twenty-one, the Jewish-born Trebitsch-Lincoln was baptized as a Lutheran in Hamburg, Germany. Soon after, he became a Presbyterian missionary in Canada. While there, he married: The son of that union professed Judaism throughout his life. Trebitsch-Lincoln, however, soon left Canada and became an Anglican curate in England. There, he became a Quaker and, in 1910, was elected a Liberal member of Parliament.

During World War I, Trebitsch-Lincoln was suspected of spying for Germany and fled to the United States. He was subsequently deported to England, convicted, and jailed for three years. By 1920, newly out of prison, he participated in an unsuccessful *putsch* against the young German republic. He escaped death by fleeing Germany, and a year later made it to China. There, he converted to Buddhism and, in 1931, was ordained a monk, taking the name Chao Kung. A year later, he became a collaborator with Japanese military intelligence in Shanghai, as well as a member of an extremist group, the Japanese Black Dragon Society. He continued working for the Japanese until his death in a Shanghai hospital in 1943. The intriguing entry on Trebitsch-Lincoln in the *Encyclopedia Judaica* (vol. 15: pp. 1364–1365) piqued the curiosity of historian Bernard Wasserstein and prompted him to write a full-scale biography of this remarkable, wandering Jew, *The Secret Lives of Trebitsch-Lincoln* (New Haven: Yale University Press, 1988).

1 "Oedipus Shmedipus, as Long as He Loves His Mother"
The Inescapable Hold of the Jewish Family

1. A wide-ranging historical and legal overview of the Fifth Commandment is found in Gerald Blidstein, *Honor Thy Father and Mother: Filial Responsibility in Jewish Law and Ethics* (New York: Ktav Publishing, 1975).

2. Chaim Bermant, *What's the Joke?: A Study of Jewish Humour Through the Ages,* pp. 150–151.

3. John Cohen, ed., *The Essential Lenny Bruce,* pp. 40–41.

2 "Two Men Come Down a Chimney"
Jewish Intelligence and the Playful Logic of the Jewish Mind

1. Ernest Van Den Haag, *The Jewish Mystique* (New York: Stein and Day, 1977), p. 15.

2. Woody Allen, *Getting Even,* p. 54.

3. The statistical overrepresentation of Jews among Nobel Prize recipients is analyzed in detail in Raphael Patai, *The Jewish Mind* (New York: Charles Scribner's Sons, 1977), pp. 339–342.

4. British scholar C. P. Snow wrote that when he was a young man, he was befriended by a powerful and intellectually vibrant Jewish family in England. When he commented once on how impressed he was by the brilliance of their social circle, the family members were displeased: "You seem to think that Jews are more intelligent

than anyone else. You must get it into perspective. We can produce Jews for you who are much stupider and much duller than anyone you can possibly believe. You just have a look at Cousin X and Aunt Y" (C. P. Snow, introduction to Arnold Rogow, ed., *The Jew in a Gentile World* [New York: Macmillan, 1961], p. XV). The family's defensive response to Snow's compliment was probably rooted, at least in part, in anxiety. It is a short step from the image of the "bright Jew" to the far less flattering image of the "crafty Jew." In similar fashion, Vance Packard, while interviewing successful non-Jewish executives and professionals for his book *The Status Seekers,* was struck by how often they referred to Jewish intelligence. Packard mentioned this to a Jewish friend, who promptly went to the library and brought Packard documentation indicating that Jews were no brighter than non-Jews (Vance Packard, *The Status Seekers* [New York: David McKay Co., 1959]), p. 275.

5. Joshua Trachtenberg, *The Devil and the Jews: The Medieval Conception of the Jew and Its Relation to Modern Antisemitism* (New Haven: Yale University Press, 1943; Cleveland and New York: Meridian Books, 1961), p. 97.

6. *Ibid.,* p. 99.

7. See Louis Rappaport, *Stalin's War Against the Jews: The Doctors' Plot and the Soviet Solution,* and Mikhail Heller and Aleksandr Nekrich, *Utopia in Power: The History of the Soviet Union from 1917 to the Present* (New York: Summit Books, 1986), pp. 502–504.

8. My version of this joke is based on Sol Jacobson, "The Logic of the Talmud," *Midstream,* vol. XXII, no. 6, June/July 1976, p. 50.

9. I have followed the translation in Hyam Maccoby, *The Day God Laughed,* p. 136.

10. *Ibid.,* p. 117.

11. I have followed the translation in Alexander Feinsilver, *The Talmud for Today* (New York: St. Martin's Press, 1980), pp. 254–255.

12. Irving Kristol, "Is Jewish Humor Dead?" *Commentary,* November 1951, p. 434.

13. *Derekh Eretz Rabbah* 1:6; cited in Hyam Maccoby, *The Day God Laughed,* p. 136.

14. With minor emendations, I have followed the wording of this story used in S. Felix Mendelsohn, *The Jew Laughs,* p. 32. Comedian Milton Berle claims that this joke represents his philosophy of life. In Berle's

version, the joke goes one stage further: "Either you're going to heaven or you're not going to heaven. If you go to heaven, there's nothing to worry about, and if you go to the other place, you'll be so doggone busy shaking hands with all your old friends, YOU WON'T HAVE TIME TO WORRY." See Lore and Maurice Cowan, *The Wit of the Jews,* p. 80.

15. Leo Rosten, *Hooray for Yiddish,* p. 86; I have somewhat altered and shortened Rosten's version. A point of trivia: Rosten also tells this story in his book *People I Have Loved, Known or Admired,* p. 65, only there, Groucho's question is, "What's the capital of *South* Dakota?"

16. Steve Allen, *Funny People,* p. 33.

17. Larry Wilde, *The Last Official Jewish Joke Book,* p. 84.

18. Khalid Kishtainy, *Arab Political Humor* (London: Quartet Books, 1985), p. 151.

19. Immanuel Olsvanger, ed., *Royte Pomerantsen,* p. XI.

20. Olsvanger, *ibid.*

3 "So How Do You Make a Hurricane?" The Jew in Business, or Jokes That Would Give an Antisemite *Nakhas*

1. For an overview of violent Jewish criminals in the United States, see Albert Fried, *The Rise and Fall of the Jewish Gangster in America* (New York: Holt, Rinehart and Winston, 1980).

2. Jackie Mason, *Jackie Mason's 'The World According to Me!'* p. 42.

3. See Salo Baron, *A Social and Religious History of the Jews* (New York: Columbia University Press, 1957), vol. 3, pp. 167–168.

4. Cited in Jacob Katz, *Exclusiveness and Tolerance: Jewish-Gentile Relations in Medieval and Modern Times* (New York: Schocken Books, 1962), p. 104.

5. While there is reason to suspect that jokes about Jews and insurance fires have generally been made up by Jews—they appear in almost every book of Jewish jokes—and are certainly laughed at by Jews, humor scholar Professor Christie Davies argues that such jokes play into deeply antisemitic stereotypes, both at the literal level—for example,

Jews are swindlers—and at the symbolic level: "An attempt to defraud an insurance company by deliberately setting a building on fire (rather than, say, faking a burglary or an accidental loss) threatens not just the profits of the insurer but also in an urban area people in that building or neighboring buildings who may get burned in the fire. Antisemitic jokes about Jews committing arson are a very specific metaphor of the general antisemitic belief in secret Jewish conspiracies that destroy people, economies, and societies so that Jews may prosper" (Christie Davis, "Jewish Jokes, Antisemitic Jokes and Hebredonian Jokes," in Avner Ziv, ed., *Jewish Humor,* p. 87). Although Davies's theory is quite provocative, he provides no proof that most such arson jokes have been made up by antisemites.

6. Leo Rosten, *The Joys of Yinglish,* pp. 228–229.

7. Milton Himmelfarb, *The Jews of Modernity* (New York: Basic Books, 1973), p. 184.

8. Lore and Maurice Cowan, *The Wit of the Jews,* p. 128.

9. This comment aside, Jack Benny, perhaps the most popular American comedian of his generation, performed little explicitly Jewish material. For Jews this was actually a blessing, since the most prominent characteristic in his comic persona was extreme stinginess, a feature that antisemitic humor has long bestowed on all Jews (for example, "How was the limbo invented?" "A Jew trying to sneak into a pay toilet."). When CBS ran a television special in February 1981, "A Love Letter to Jack Benny," the comedian was shown in an old clip explaining why his show was not really a special: "To me a special is when coffee goes from eighty-five cents a pound to seventy-four cents." In Benny's most famous radio routine, a robber's voice is heard saying to him, "Your money or your life!" There is a long pause, until the robber says, "Well?" and Benny responds: "I'm thinking, I'm thinking."

10. Jackie Mason, *Jackie Mason's 'The World According to Me!'* p. 73.

11. Henny Youngman with Neal Karlen, *Take My Life, Please,* p. 45.

12. Most wealthy Jews have recollections of parents or grandparents who lived in dire poverty, and in the case of the late billionaire and Eastern European refugee Robert Maxwell, the pattern of poverty, extraordinary wealth, and bankruptcy can be seen in one generation.

13. Andrew M. Greeley, *Ethnicity, Denomination, and Inequality* (Beverly Hills, Calif.: 1976), p. 39.

14. Cited in Seymour Martin Lipset, ed., *American Pluralism and the Jewish Community* (New Brunswick, N.J.: Transaction Publishers, 1990), p. 3.

15. Reported in Barry Kosmin, "The Dimensions of Contemporary Jewish Philanthropy," unpublished paper, North American Jewish Data Bank, Graduate School, City University of New York, 1988, p. 13.

16. With minor variations, this joke is told by William Novak and Moshe Waldoks, *The Big Book of Jewish Humor,* p. 264. More than the name Plotnick, what makes this joke quintessentially Jewish is its overriding conviction that justice must prevail. When the patriarch Abraham thinks that God is acting improperly, he has no compunction about challenging Him in the name of morality: "Shall not the judge of all the earth act with justice?" (Genesis 18:25). In another biblical verse, the obsession with justice is formally codified: "Justice, justice you shall pursue" (Deuteronomy 16:20).

The "Plotnick Diamond" is about justice's insistence that injustice be punished. The sexy young woman obviously married Plotnick for his wealth; in the Jewish tradition, such marriages are denounced in the strongest terms: "He who marries for money," the Talmud teaches, "will have evil children" (presumably like him or herself; *Kiddushin* 70a). Elsewhere, it warns that one who marries his daughter off to an old, presumably rich, man causes her to become a whore (*Sanhedrin* 76a); frustration will likely cause her to commit adultery.

In this joke, justice's victory over greed is obvious. The sexy young woman married for money. Now she's paying for it.

4 "The Doctor Is Three and the Lawyer Is Two" Self-loathing, Self-praise, and Other Jewish Neuroses

1. Jackie Mason, *Jackie Mason's 'The World According to Me!'* p. 42.

2. A classic nineteenth-century Eastern European joke simultaneously mocks Jewish aversion to physical confrontations and gentile jingoism:

A group of yeshiva bucherim [students] are drafted into the army, and to everyone's amazement become crack shots. They're sent to the front. The enemy soon attacks, and the captain orders them to fire, but not a trigger is pulled. As the enemy troops draw closer, the captain repeats the order at the top of his lungs. To no avail.

"What's wrong with you?" he yells at the soldiers. "I told you to fire."

"What are you talking about?" one of the yeshiva students answers. "Don't you see? Those are men out there. If we shoot, someone might get hurt."

When told among Eastern European and American Jews, the primary target of the joke is the warrior ethos of the gentile world. Among Jews who have had to fight, however, it is the shlemiel-like nature of the yeshiva students that is more apt to be mocked. In Primo Levi's *If Not Now, When?*, a novel about Jewish anti-Nazi fighters, members of a partisan band are discussing the morality of stalking retreating Nazi troops, when one of them tells the foregoing joke. Another partisan walks in as the storyteller is finishing.

Ulybin was about thirty, of medium height, muscular and dark: He had an oval face, impassive, always freshly shaven.

"Well, why don't you go on? Let's hear the ending," Ulybin said.

Pavel resumed, with less confidence and less gusto. "Then one of the [yeshiva] students says, 'Can't you see, Captain, sir? They aren't cardboard outlines, they're men, like us. If we shoot, we might hurt them.'"

The partisans around the table ventured some hesitant little laughs, looking from Pavel to Ulybin. Ulybin said, "I didn't hear the beginning. Who were these men who didn't want to shoot?"

Pavel gave him a fairly sketchy summary of the beginning of the joke, and Ulybin asked, in an icy voice, "And you here, what would you all do?"

There was a brief silence, then Mendel's soft voice was heard, "We're not yeshiva bucherim."

(Primo Levi, *If Not Now, When?* [New York: Summit Books, 1985], p. 116; see also the discussion and analysis of this joke in Paul Breines, *Tough Jews: Political Fantasies and the Moral Dilemma of American Jewry* [New York: Basic Books, 1990], pp. 136–137).

3. *Vanity Fair,* March 1991, p. 228; *Forbes* (special issue, "The 400 Richest People in America," 1991 edition, p. 196) estimates Geffen's worth at a minimum of $880 million.

4. "That the Jews had horns and tails," writes M. Hirsh Goldberg, "emanated from the Christian belief that since the Jews killed Christ, they either were in league with the devil or were incarnations of the devil himself, complete therefore with Satan's horns and tail" (*Just Because They're Jewish* [New York: Stein and Day, 1979], p. 28). The belief that Jews had horns was given additional "confirmation" by Michelangelo's sculpture of Moses the Lawgiver, in which the greatest of Hebrew prophets is depicted with two horns coming out of his head. Michelangelo's error was less likely rooted in antisemitism than in a faulty Greek translation of the Torah. Exodus 34:35 speaks of *karan* (rays of light) shining forth from Moses' forehead, but the earliest Greek translation of the Torah rendered *karan* as if it were *keren,* the Hebrew word for horns. Whether attributable to the satanic view of the Jews or to Michelangelo's *Moses,* the notion that Jews have horns took hold of the popular imagination, reaching from Europe to rural parts of the United States. Historian Joshua Trachtenberg, author of *The Devil and the Jews* (New Haven: Yale University Press, 1943), a study in medieval Christianity's perception of the Jews, reported that "on a trip through Kansas ... I met a farmer who refused to believe that I was Jewish because there were no horns on my head. And I have since learned that this experience is not uncommon."

5. Cited in Steve Allen, *More Funny People,* p. 245.

6. See William Helmreich, *The Things They Say Behind Your Back: Stereotypes and the Myths Behind Them* (New York: Doubleday, 1982), pp. 35–37.

7. Rodney Dangerfield, *I Don't Get No Respect* (Los Angeles: Price/Stern/Sloan, 1982), n.p.

8. *Tosefta Terumot* 7:23 teaches: "If heathen said to a company of men: 'Give us one of you that we kill him or else we will kill all of you,' they should all let themselves be killed rather than deliver a single soul in Israel. But if they specified a certain person, as they specified Sheba, son of Bichri (II Samuel 20:1–22), they should not allow themselves to be killed and should hand him over." Since Sheba, son of Bichri, was a rebel against King David, the implication of the ruling is that unless the person specified is guilty of a capital or very serious crime, a group should not hand over someone who is undeserving of death to be killed, even if as a result many innocent people in the group might die. See the discussion of this ruling in Louis Jacob, *Jewish Law* (New York: Behrman House, 1968), pp. 82–83.

9. Freud's version of the joke, in *Jokes and their Relation to the Unconscious,* is found on pp. 49–50.

10. Alan Dershowitz, *Chutzpah* (Boston: Little, Brown, 1991), p. 18.

11. Robert Hendrickson, *The Facts on File Encyclopedia of Word and Phrase Origins* (New York: Facts on File Publications, 1987), p. 118.

12. Alan Dershowitz, *op. cit.*, p. 18.

13. Folklorist Gene Bluestein suggests that the Yiddish meaning of *shmuck* might well have derived from the German and refers to "the family jewels, a well-known euphemism for the male genitals" (Gene Bluestein, *Anglish/Yiddish: Yiddish in American Life and Literature* [Athens, Ga.: University of Georgia Press, 1989]), p. 89.

14. Reported in Gene Bluestein, *op. cit.*, p. 90.

15. Leo Rosten, *The Joys of Yiddish*, pp. 361–362.

16. There were those who did not share traditional Judaism's enthusiasm about sex, the medieval rabbi and philosopher Moses Maimonides (1135–1204) being the most prominent. Maimonides, who was also a physician, claimed that most people die from sexual overindulgence. One finds similar negativism in several other Jewish scholars, particularly in the medieval period; nonetheless, "a completely negative attitude [toward sexuality] was impossible since Judaism teaches that it is a religious duty to marry" (Louis Jacobs, *What Does Judaism Say About...?* [Jerusalem: Keter Publishing House, 1973], p. 281). Already at the time of the Talmud, Jewish law ruled that if a husband suddenly turned celibate, his wife could petition the court to force him either to resume relations or to grant her a divorce.

17. An appreciation of the sensual is a dominant theme in the Song of Songs, and is expressed both by the young female shepherdess and by the man who loves her. "Oh, give me the kisses of your mouth," the second verse reads. "For your love is more delightful than wine." "Your lips are like a crimson thread, Your mouth is lovely. ... Your breasts are like two fawns, twins of a gazelle. ... Every part of you is fair, my darling. There is no blemish in you" (4:3,5,7). "His mouth is delicious, and all of him is delightful. Such is my beloved, such is my darling" (5:16). "Your stately form is like the palm, your breasts are like clusters. I say: 'Let me climb the palm, let me take hold of its branches. Let your breasts be like clusters of grapes, your breath like the fragrance of apples, and your mouth like the choicest wine'" (7:8–10).

18. The frank treatment of sexual matters in the Bible provided ample

material for jokesters. Sigmund Freud, as untraditional a Jew as has ever lived, told the following to his friend and disciple Theodor Reik:

> *The boy Itzig is asked in grammar school: "Who was Moses?"*
> *"Moses was the son of an Egyptian princess."*
> *"That's not true," says the teacher. "Moses was the son of a Hebrew mother. The Egyptian princess found the baby in a casket."*
> *But Itzig answers: "Says she."*

This joke, as infuriating to traditional Jews as a joke claiming that Jesus' father was a Roman soldier would be to Christians, was told by Freud about 1908, and illustrates that humor is often not just a laughing matter. Some thirty years after Freud started relating this joke, he wrote his most controversial book, *Moses and Monotheism,* whose thesis is contained in the joke. Moses was an Egyptian, Freud argued, not a Jew, and monotheism—generally regarded as Judaism's greatest contribution to the world—was not a Jewish but an Egyptian creation. The joke, originally told in Theodor Reik, "Freud and Jewish Wit," in *Psychoanalysis* 2:12–20 (1954), serves as the opening lines in an important work of contemporary scholarship, Yosef Hayim Yerushalmi, *Freud's Moses: Judaism Terminable and Interminable* (New Haven: Yale University Press, 1991), p. 1.

19. Quoted in Kenneth Tynan, *Show People: Profiles in Entertainment,* p. 191.

20. Henny Youngman with Neal Karlen, *Take My Life, Please,* p. 178.

21. On the fights between the Hasidim and their opponents, and the relatively minor ritual innovations of the Hasidim, see Jacob Katz, *Tradition and Crisis* (New York: Schocken Books, 1971), pp. 231–244; and Mordecai Wilensky, "Hasidic-Mitnaggedic Polemics in the Jewish Communities of Eastern Europe: The Hostile Phase," in Gerson David Hundert, ed., *Essential Papers on Hasidism: Origins to Present* (New York: New York University Press, 1991), pp. 244–271.

22. Because Jewish law plays a less significant role within Conservative Judaism than in Orthodox Judaism, fights inside Conservative congregations are more apt to focus on personal rather than legal issues. Most commonly, they revolve around the rabbi's personality. In one prominent congregation in the 1970s, an ex-president of the synagogue heard rumors that the rabbi was having an affair

with a married woman. Realizing that he might finally have found the pretext for having the rabbi, whom he hated, fired from a lifetime contract, the ex-president hired detectives to follow him. The rumors proved to be true, and less than twenty-four hours after the ex-president presented photographic evidence of the rabbi's affair before the synagogue's board, the rabbi's name was off the synagogue's stationery.

In one wealthy southern congregation, the rabbi was popular, but the president had bitter enemies. When the man ran for reelection, the opposing candidate sent a letter to the synagogue membership accusing the president of using "Stalin-like" tactics in running the congregation. As absurd as such charges sound to outsiders—Stalin murdered more than twenty million people in the Gulag Archipelago; the "crime" of the synagogue's president was that he had kept his opponent off the congregation's ritual committee—such verbal overkill is common in Jewish communal life.

During the 1940s, the issue that prompted the most vicious fights within Reform synagogues was Zionism. Certain Reform congregations, claiming that Judaism was solely a religion, and that the Jews were not a people, were fanatically anti-Zionist. In an action that today would be deemed antisemitic, several congregations barred Jews who contributed to the United Jewish Appeal from synagogue membership. After Israel's creation in 1948, Zionism ceased to be controversial, and fights shifted to the more traditional frontier—the rabbi's personality.

23. A critical discussion by an *Orthodox* rabbi of the tendency to see the *mezuzah* as a protective amulet is found in Rabbi Martin Gordon, "Mezuzah: Protective Amulet or Religious Symbol?," *Tradition,* Summer 1977, pp. 7–40.

24. See H. J. Zimmels, *Ashkenazim and Sephardim: Their Relations, Differences and Problems as Reflected in the Rabbinical Responsa* (London: Oxford University Press, 1958), p. 62.

25. See Howard Faulkner and Virginia Pruitt, eds., *The Selected Correspondence of Karl A. Menninger* (New Haven: Yale University Press, 1988), p. 282; cited in Sander Gilman, *The Jew's Body* (New York and London: Routledge, 1991), p. 26.

26. See Joe Singer, *How to Curse in Yiddish;* William Novak and Moshe Waldoks, *The Big Book of Jewish Humor,* pp. 152–153; and Lore and Maurice Cowan, *The Wit of the Jews,* p. 93.

5 "Pardon Me, Do You Have Another Globe?" Persecution and the Jewish Sense of Homelessness

1. In recent years, research has revealed that the Allies bombed Auschwitz twice in the summer of 1944, but they had such accurate maps' of the camp that they were able to restrict their bombings to the rubber factories, where inmates did forced labor for the Germans, while leaving the gas chambers and train tracks leading to Auschwitz undamaged. See David Wyman, *The Abandonment of the Jews: America and the Holocaust 1941–1945* (New York: Pantheon, 1984), and Martin Gilbert, *Auschwitz and the Allies* (New York: Holt, Rinehart and Winston, 1981).

2. Lore and Maurice Cowan, *The Wit of the Jews,* p. 126.

3. These three libels, that Jews killed non-Jews and drank their blood, that Jews poisoned the wells of Europe, and that Jews desecrated the wafer, are discussed in Dennis Prager and Joseph Telushkin, *Why the Jews? The Reason for Antisemitism* (New York: Simon and Schuster, 1983), pp. 97–103; see also Joshua Trachtenberg, *The Devil and the Jews: The Medieval Conception of the Jew and Its Relation to Modern Antisemitism* (New Haven, Yale University Press, 1943; Cleveland and New York: Meridian Books), pp. 97–155.

4. An annotated translation of three of the most famous Jewish-Christian disputations is found in Hyam Maccoby, *Judaism on Trial: Jewish-Christian Disputations in the Middle Ages* (Rutherford, N.J.: Fairleigh Dickinson University Press, div. of Associated University Presses, 1982).

5. S. Felix Mendelsohn, *The Jew Laughs,* p. 46. This twentieth-century joke, with its claim that antisemites will kill Jews with or without provocation, seems to be a witty reworking of an unfunny story the talmudic rabbis tell about the second-century Roman emperor Hadrian: "A certain Jew happened to be walking in the street when the emperor rode by. The Jew greeted him.

"'Who are you?' asked Hadrian.

"'I am a Jew,' answered the man.

"The emperor flew into a rage. 'How dare a Jew greet me! Let him be executed for his impudence.'

"The next day, another Jew chanced to be walking as the emperor went by. The man had learned of the fate of the first Jew and did not dare greet the emperor. Hadrian again showed his anger. 'Who are you?' he demanded.

"The man answered: 'I am a Jew.'

"Hadrian then shouted: 'What impudence of this fellow to walk past me and not acknowledge me. Let him be executed for his disrespect.'

"His counselors then said: 'Sire, we do not understand your policy; yesterday a man was executed for greeting you and today another man is executed for not greeting you.'

"Hadrian replied, 'Why do you try to teach me how to behave toward my enemies. Whatever they do is wrong.'" (*Lamentations Rabbah* 3:41).

6. See Paul Lendvai, *Anti-Semitism Without Jews: Communist Eastern Europe* (Garden City, N.Y.: Doubleday, 1971).

7. Steven Lukes and Itzhak Galnoor, *No Laughing Matter: A Collection of Political Jokes,* pp. 27–28.

8. Yaffa Eliach, *Hasidic Tales of the Holocaust* (New York: Oxford University Press, 1982), pp. 142–147.

9. Isaac Asimov, *Treasury of Humor,* p. 269.

10. Menachem Begin's attitudes toward Germany are discussed in Ze'ev Chafets, *Heroes and Hard Hats, Hustlers and Holy Men: Inside the New Israel* (New York: William Morrow, 1986), pp. 104–105.

11. Quoted in Maurice Yacover, *In Method of Madness: The Comic Art of Mel Brooks* (New York: St. Martin's Press, 1981), p. 17.

12. Lore and Maurice Cowan, *The Wit of the Jews,* p. 104.

13. Seymour Martin Lipset, "A Unique People in an Exceptional Century," in Seymour Martin Lipset, ed., *American Pluralism and the Jewish Community* (New Brunswick, N.J.: Transaction Publishers, 1990), p. 22. Lipset goes on to note that Jewish "lack of confidence in the larger community goes beyond concern with antisemitism." A national survey conducted by the National Opinion Research Center in 1964 revealed that Jews are much less trustful of people in general than members of seven other white ethnic groups: Irish, Scandinavians, Slavs, German Protestants, German Catholics, Italians, and WASPs. "On a scale created from answers to six questions, running from plus 4 (total trust) to minus 4 (total distrust), Jews scored on the average minus 3. No other group was in the minus range. The questions included items such as 'Do you think most

people can be trusted?' and 'If you don't watch out, people will take advantage of you'" (p. 22).

14. Larry Wilde, *The Complete Book of Ethnic Humor*, p. 51.

15. *The New York Times*, February 16, 1930, quoting an address Einstein gave at the Sorbonne in Paris, in December 1929.

16. See Robert Conquest, *The Great Terror: Stalin's Purge of the Thirties* (New York: Macmillan, revised edition, 1973).

17. C. Bane and Alan Dundes, *You Call This Living? A Collection of East European Political Jokes*, p. 162. In Bane and Dundes's version, the final line reads: "Damn those dirty kikes, they've been favored as usual by being warned first."

18. Steven Lukes and Itzhak Galnoor, *No Laughing Matter: A Collection of Political Jokes*, pp. 163–164.

6 "And I Used to Be a Hunchback" Assimilation and Its Delusions

1. The application of this dictum ("even if he sins, he remains a Jew") to apostates was not the original intention of the Talmud, but the innovative teaching of Rashi, the greatest medieval Bible and Talmud commentator. See the discussion of this dictum in Jacob Katz, *Exclusiveness and Tolerance: Jewish-Gentile Relations in Medieval and Modern Times* (New York: Schocken Books, 1961), pp. 69–72.

2. A discussion of the Jewish population in the Roman Empire is found in Salo Baron, *A Social and Religious History of the Jews* (New York: Columbia University Press, 2nd ed., 1952), vol. II, pp. 370–372.

3. See Chaim Greenberg, *The Inner Eye, Volume II* (New York: Jewish Frontier Publishing Association, 1964), pp. 229–243. "When Trotsky escaped from his Siberian exile in 1902," Greenberg notes, "some associates at a small railway station gave him some clothing and a blank passport. On his way to Samara he had to fill out the passport. When he came to the choice of a name he did not give the matter much thought and put down the name of the chief supervisor of the Odessa prison where he had been jailed for some months. Why did he choose the name of a supervisor of a jail?" (p. 237). Greenberg speculates that at a subconscious level, Trotsky, a supporter of totalitarianism, identified with the jailer. Which is why, even after the Communists came to power and Trotsky was named head of the Red Army,

he never took back his Jewish name. Ironically, David Axelrod, a great-grandson of Trotsky, emigrated to Israel in the 1980s, where he became a prominent follower of the late Meir Kahane, the most *right-wing* figure in Israeli politics (*Jerusalem Report,* October 3, 1991, p. 8).

4. A man of his word, David Selznick, agreed to co-sponsor a fund-raising event with Hecht. See Ben Hecht, *A Child of the Century* (New York: Simon and Schuster, 1954), pp. 539–545; cited in Neal Gabler, *An Empire of Their Own: How the Jews Invented Hollywood* (New York: Crown, 1988), pp. 290–291.

5. Sol Liptzin, ed. and trans., *Peretz* (New York, 1947), pp. 266–275; there is a particularly insightful discussion of Peretz's story by Benjamin Kahn, "Freedom and Identity: The Challenge of Modernity," in Alfred Jospe, ed., *Tradition and Contemporary Experience: Essay on Jewish Thought and Life* (New York: Schocken Books, 1970), pp. 15–16. Although Liptzin's book is no longer in print, the Peretz story has been reprinted in Jack Riemer and Nathaniel Stampfer, eds., *So That Your Values Live On—Ethical Wills and How to Prepare Them* (Woodstock, Vt.: Jewish Lights Publishing, 1991), pp. 217–222.

6. Herman Wouk, *This Is My God* (Boston: Little, Brown, 1959); Wouk's impassioned plea against Jewish assimilation is found on pp. 229–235.

7. In his essay *On the Jewish Question,* Karl Marx described Jews and Judaism in Nazi-like language: "What is the secular cult of the Jew? *Haggling.* What is his secular god? *Money.* Well, then! Emancipation from *haggling* and *money,* from practical, real Judaism, would be the self-emancipation of our time.... Money is the jealous God of Israel, beside which no other God may stand" (Quintin Hoare, ed., and Rodney Livingstone and Gregor Benton, trans., Karl Marx, *Early Writings* [New York: Random House, Vintage Books, 1975], pp. 236, 239). Marx's antisemitism did Jews particular damage, since his readers, knowing that he was born a Jew, probably assumed that what he wrote about Jews must be accurate. Hitler himself claimed to have been influenced by this widely distributed essay: "It is quite enough that the scientific knowledge of the danger of Judaism is gradually deepened and that every individual on the basis of this knowledge begins to eliminate the Jew within himself, and I am very much afraid that this beautiful thought originates from none other than a Jew" (cited in Julius Carlebach, *Karl Marx and the Radical Critique of Judaism* [London: Routledge and Kegan Paul, 1978], pp. 355–356).

8. The mind-set of nineteenth-century Jewish apostates is described in Michael Meyer, *The Origins of the Modern Jew: Jewish Identity and European Culture in Germany, 1749–1824* (Detroit: Wayne State University Press, 1967).

9. Ernst L. Freud, ed., *The Letters of Sigmund Freud and Arnold Zweig,* translated by Elaine and William Robson-Scott, p. 3.

10. See Edward Norden, "Counting the Jews," *Commentary,* October 1991, pp. 36–43.

11. *Ibid.,* p. 42. One reason for the steep decline in conversions to Judaism is Reform Judaism's decision to change the definition of who is a Jew. According to traditional Jewish law, a Jew is one who is born to a Jewish mother or who converts to Judaism. Since a majority of intermarriages involve a Jewish man marrying a non-Jewish woman, there has long been considerable pressure on the woman to convert, since unless she does, the couple's children will not be Jews. In 1983, the Central Conference of American [Reform] Rabbis ruled that any child with one Jewish parent, who had been raised with a Jewish identity, would be regarded as Jewish. This decision reduced the pressure on a non-Jewish woman marrying a Jewish man to convert, since her non-Jewishness need no longer keep the children from being accepted as Jews. The decline in the number of converts since 1983 has been marked.

12. There is one more joke in which the term *shiksa* figures prominently:

> *An Orthodox rabbi angrily berates his son:*
> *"They say you are going out with* shiksas.*"*
> *"But it's not true," the son says.*
> *"Bad enough they say it. It should be true also?" the father*
> *answers.*

7 "If I Could Just See One Miracle"
Poking Fun At God, His Law, and His Spokesmen on Earth

1. Woody Allen, "Selections from the Allen Notebooks," in Woody Allen, *Without Feathers,* p. 10.

2. Quoted in Eric Lax, *On Being Funny: Woody Allen and Comedy*, p. 232.

3. Leo Rosten, *The Joys of Yinglish*, p. 273.

4. Jewish scholars generally cite three messianic episodes that, from the Jewish perspective, were unfortunate. In the first century of the Common Era, the followers of Jesus inaugurated a new religion in his name. A hundred years later, in 132, Simon Bar-Kokhba, a military leader in Judea, proclaimed himself to be the Messiah and started a revolt against Rome. By the time the Romans quelled the revolt in 135, more than half a million Jews were dead and tens of thousands of Jewish men and women had been sold off in Roman markets as slaves and prostitutes. In the seventeenth century, more than half of world Jewry believed that a Turkish Jew, Shabbetai Zevi, was the Messiah. Shabbetai announced that he would confront the sultan of Turkey and reclaim Palestine for the Jews. Records exist of Jewish communities in England laying ten-to-one odds that all Jews would be transferred to Palestine within two years. (I have long wondered how they planned to collect on the bets from their new abodes.) In Germany, rich Jews sold their possessions and stored food and other valuables in large barrels, which they intended to take on their messianic journey. Unfortunately, Shabbetai's meeting with the sultan did not come off. Instead, the sultan sent the self-styled Messiah word that, unless he converted to Islam, he would be executed. Shabbetai donned the fez, thereby ending the unhappy history of yet another Jewish messiah. In light of their repeated bad experiences with messiahs, many rabbis became decidedly sober on the whole subject. See Hyam Maccoby, *Revolution in Judaea* (New York: Taplinger, 1980); Yehoshafat Harkabi, *The Bar-Kokhba Syndrome: Risk and Realism in International Politics* (New York: Rossel Books, 1983); Gershom Scholem, *Sabbatai Sevi: The Mystical Messiah 1626–1676* (New Jersey: Princeton University Press, 1973).

5. *Avot d'Rabbi Nathan*, version B, chapter 31, Schechter edition.

6. Jerusalem Talmud, *Ta'anit* 4:8, 68d.

7. Woody Allen, "The Scrolls," in Woody Allen, *Without Feathers*, p. 28.

8. A similar version of the story, with minor variations, is told in Nathan Ausubel, ed., *A Treasury of Jewish Folklore*, p. 36.

9. Thus, if an Orthodox Jew tells a joke about a rabbi, the butt of the joke is most likely to be a Reform rabbi. The exception is jokes that the *Mitnagdim* (Orthodox Jewish rationalists) tell about Hasidic *rebbes*. In one story:

A Hasid is telling a friend about a miracle that he personally witnessed. His rebbe was standing on the street, speaking to some of his followers, and a Mitnaggid *was standing nearby, mocking everything the* rebbe *said. Finally, the* rebbe *could take it no longer. "May that wall near the* Mitnaggid," *he pronounced, "collapse and fall down upon him."*

"But Rebbe," *one of his followers enjoined. "The wall is very tall. If it falls down, other, innocent, people will be hurt, not just the* Mitnaggid."

"You're right," the rebbe *said. "May that wall not fall down."*

"And would you believe it," the Hasid relating the story concluded, "the wall just stayed in its place?"

Rabbi Eliezer Shakh is regarded as the leader of the *Mitnagdim* in Israel today, and in the mid-1980s, the following joke circulated in Israel:

Rabbi Shakh was asked: "If you had to be born again and couldn't be born as a Jew, what would you prefer to be born as?"

Rabbi Shakh was quiet for a long while. "If I couldn't be born as a Jew," he finally said, "then I would prefer to be born as a Lubavitcher Hasid."

An Orthodox rabbi who shows such contempt for other Orthodox Jews is inconsistent with the popular assumption that Orthodoxy is monolithic. In reality, the schisms within Orthodoxy have often been even more bitter than the current divisions between Orthodox and Reform Jews.

10. Told in Rabbi S. Y. Zevin, *A Treasury of Chassidic Tales on the Torah* (New York: Mesorah Publications, 1980), pp. 189–191.

11. See Richard Rubenstein, "A Rabbi Dies," in Jacob Neusner, *American Judaism: Adventure in Modernity* (Englewood Cliffs, N.J.: Prentice-Hall, Inc., 1972), pp. 46–59, see especially p. 56.

12. In an even earlier story, contained in the thirteenth-century *Book of the Pious (Sefer Hasidim),* a Jewishly illiterate shepherd offered his own prayer to God: "Lord of the World! It is apparent and known to You that if You had cattle and gave them to me to tend, although I take wages for tending from all others, from You I would take nothing, because I love You."

A learned man overheard the shepherd's prayer, and said to him, "Fool, this is not the way to pray."

"How should I pray?" the shepherd asked.

The learned man taught him the traditional prayers in the right order, the blessings, the *Sh'ma* ("Hear, O Israel, the Lord is our God, the Lord is One"), and the other major prayers.

After the learned man left, the shepherd forgot all the new prayers he had been taught and stopped praying. He was even afraid to say the old prayer, since the learned man had told him not to. One night, the learned man had a dream in which a voice told him: "If you do not tell the shepherd to say the prayer he used to say, misfortune will come upon you, for you have robbed me of one who belongs to the world-to-come."

The learned man sought out the shepherd and said to him: "What prayer are you now saying?"

"None," the shepherd answered, "for I have forgotten the prayers you taught me, and you forbade me to say my usual words."

The learned man told him about his dream and added, "Say what you used to say!" (cited in Lionel Blue with Jonathan Magonet, *The Blue Guide to the Here and Hereafter* [London: Collins, 1988], p. 192).

13. For the significance of charity in Jewish life, see Jacob Neusner, *Tzedakah,* as well as my *Jewish Literacy* (New York: William Morrow, 1991), pp. 511–514.

14. Jack Riemer, "A Serious Look at Modern Jewish Humor," an unpublished paper by the author, p. 24.

15. Several years ago, I had just finished making a fund-raising appeal in Los Angeles when a member of the audience announced that because the Jewish Federation publicized the names of donors, he had no wish to give to the campaign. Hearing more than a few murmured assents, I said: "Suppose I told you that near me in Israel [where I was then living] lives a family of Ethiopian Jews who succeeded in escaping, but who left five members behind in Ethiopia. Because of starvation and antisemitic attacks, these five people's lives are in imminent danger. If I can raise twenty-five thousand dollars, we will be able to bribe the right people in Ethiopia and get these people out. And because this is a matter of life or death, I am going to call out the name of each person in this room and ask you to stand and announce what you are giving." Or, I said, "Since I don't want to embarrass anyone, after I finish I will leave a box up here, and ask each of you to please put in what you can. How many of you," I asked, "would give more if you were called by name, and how many would give the same if your gift was anonymous?" On this and subsequent occasions,

I discovered that generally about 60 percent of respondents say they would give more if their names were called out than if they were giving anonymously. That, of course, is why charitable organizations publicize the names of donors.

16. Chaim Bermant, *The Jews* (New York: Times Books, 1977), p. 199. In the British-Jewish community of the nineteenth and early twentieth century, Bermant claims, when rabbis piously intoned, "The Lord will provide," they generally meant, Lord Rothschild. In a recent article on "The Problem of Plaques," Rabbi Louis Jacobs notes that publicizing names of donors on synagogue plaques "acts as an encouragement for people to give money and gifts to synagogue needs," while simultaneously catering to "a *mild* form of vanity" (emphasis mine). According to Jacobs, rabbinic sources have long recognized the existence of such vanity, and instead of trying to destroy it, the rabbis choose to try and manipulate it to influence people to do good. Hence, if it is important to many people to become famous, then let them strive to become famous for doing good deeds. Thus, the Torah records that Joseph's brothers decided to sell him into slavery: "But when Reuben [his oldest brother] heard it, he tried to save him from them" (Genesis 37:21). Comments the Midrash: "Had Reuben known that Scripture would record of him, 'But when Reuben heard it...' he would have carried Joseph on his shoulders back to his father." Similarly, the Book of Ruth records that the wealthy farmer Boaz fed the impoverished Ruth "roasted grain, and she ate her fill and had some left over" (2:14). Concerning which, the Midrash comments: "Had Boaz known that Scripture would record of him, 'And he handed her roasted grain...' he would have fed her with fatted calves" (*Midrash Rabbah, Ruth* 5:6).

17. Isaac Asimov, *Treasury of Humor,* p. 239.

18. *Ibid.,* p. 240.

8 "Better to Be Late in This World Than Early in the Next" Why Are There So Few Funny Israeli Jokes?

1. On *The Tonight Show,* July 24, 1970; cited in Sig Altman, *The Comic Image of the Jew,* p. 91.

2. Cited in Michael Bar-Zohar, *Ben-Gurion: A Biography* (New York: Delacorte, 1978), p. 303.

3. Thomas Friedman, *From Beirut to Jerusalem* (New York: Farrar, Straus and Giroux, 1989), pp. 76–105.

4. From Golda Meir's autobiography, *My Life,* and cited by Israel Shenker, "Golda Meir," in Arthur Gelb, A. M. Rosenthal, and Marvin Siegel, eds., *The New York Times Great Lives of the Twentieth Century* (New York: Times Books, 1988), p. 463.

5. Ze'ev Chafets, *Heroes and Hard Hats, Hustlers and Holy Men* (New York: William Morrow, 1986), p. 216. Chafets's book is the best work I know of describing day-to-day life in Israel.

9 "Why Is This Knight Different from All Other Knights" Seven Final—and Unrelated—Jewish Jokes

1. Leo Rosten, *Hooray for Yiddish!,* p. 251.

2. See Steve Allen, *Funny People,* pp. 24–29, where the Woody-moose routine is printed and discussed.

3. A responsa by Rabbi Ezekiel Landau condemning hunting is translated in Solomon Freehof, *The Responsa Literature and A Treasury of Responsa* (New York: Ktav Publishing, 1973), pp. 216–219.

Annotated Bibliography

▶

Allen, Steve. *Funny People*. New York: Stein and Day, 1981. Although Allen had no intention of focusing on Jewish humor in this analysis of America's leading comedians, most of the comedians he discusses are Jews. Among those discussed are Woody Allen, Mel Brooks, Billy Crystal, Sid Caesar, Lenny Bruce, and Groucho Marx. In a sequel, *More Funny People* (New York: Stein and Day, 1982), Allen examines the humor of Jack Benny, Allan Sherman, and Jerry Lewis among others.

Allen, Woody. *Getting Even*. New York: Warner Books, 1971.
———. *Side Effects*. New York: Random House, 1980.
———. *Without Feathers*. New York: Warner Books, 1975. Allen clearly has mixed feelings about his Jewishness. On the one hand, Jews who are committed to Jewish survival and who therefore oppose intermarriage arouse his wrath. "Is there anything uglier," he asks in one essay, "than families that don't want their children to marry loved ones because they're of the wrong religion?" ("Random Reflections of a Second-Rate Mind," in Joyce Carol Oates, ed., *The Best American Essays 1991* [New York: Ticknor and Fields, 1991], p. 3). On the other, he has responded wittily to the accusation that he despises his own Jewishness: "I have frequently been accused of being a self-hating Jew, and while it's true I am Jewish and I don't like myself very much, it's not because of my persuasion" (*ibid.*, p. 5). While not particularly knowledgeable about Judaism, Allen has an uncanny ear for religious pretentiousness. Consider this takeoff (in *Without Feathers*) on pompously worded English-language translations of the Bible:

> *And it came to pass that a man who sold shirts was smitten by hard times. Neither did any of his merchandise move nor did he prosper. And he prayed and said, "Lord, why hast Thou left me to suffer thus? All mine enemies sell their goods except I. And it's the height of the season. My shirts are good shirts. Take a look at this rayon. I got button-downs, flare collars, nothing sells. Yet I have kept Thy commandments. Why can I not earn a living when mine younger brother cleans up in children's ready-to-wear?"*

And the Lord heard the man and said: "About thy shirts . . ."
"Yes, Lord," the man said, falling to his knees.
"Put an alligator over the pocket."
"Pardon me, Lord?"
"Just do what I'm telling you. You won't be sorry."
And the man sewed onto all his shirts a small alligator symbol and
lo and behold, suddenly his merchandise moved like gangbusters, and
there was much rejoicing while amongst his enemies there was wailing
and gnashing of teeth, and one said, "The Lord is merciful. He maketh me
to lie down in green pastures. The problem is, I can't get up."

Along with these three collections of comic essays, there are a large number of books analyzing Allen's humor, particularly that in his films. Most also evaluate the Jewish component in his work. Particularly significant are two recent works, *Woody Allen: A Biography,* by Eric Lax (New York: Knopf, 1991), and *Woody Allen,* by Graham McCann (Cambridge, England: Polity Press, 1990). See also, Foster Hirsch, *Love, Sex, Death, and the Meaning of Life: Woody Allen's Comedy* (New York: Limelight Editions, 1990); Diane Jacobs, *But We Need the Eggs: The Magic of Woody Allen* (New York: St. Martin's Press, 1982); Eric Lax, *On Being Funny: Woody Allen and Comedy* (New York: Charterhouse, 1975); Gerald McKnight, *Woody Allen: Joking Aside* (London: W. H. Allen, 1982); and Maurice Yacowar, *Loser Takes All: The Comic Art of Woody Allen* (New York: Frederick Ungar Publishing Co., 1979).

Altman, Sig. *The Comic Image of the Jew: Explorations of a Pop Culture Phenomenon.* Rutherford, N.J.: Fairleigh Dickinson University Press, 1971. In modern American culture, the word "comic" goes with "Jewish" like the word "Irish" goes with "cop"; Altman is insightful in explaining how this has come about, while also documenting how Jewish humor has penetrated American life. His book contains some unusual lists; e.g., all Broadway plays between 1964 and 1970 that had a Jewish component. During the 1967–1968 season, for example, there were twelve (see pp. 206–217). Altman's chapter on Jews as comic figures on television talk shows (pp. 71–99) is particularly interesting. However, the funniest line in the book is the one that Altman heard from Catholic actor Pat O'Brien on *The Merv Griffin Show*: "The priest was saying, 'Every man in this parish must die one day.' A little man kept laughing. Finally, the priest asked him, 'And why are you laughing?' 'I'm not from this parish,' the little man said."

Asimov, Isaac. *Treasury of Humor.* Boston: Houghton Mifflin, 1971. A collection of Asimov's 640 favorite jokes. While they encompass many subjects, the longest chapter is devoted to Jewish humor (pp.

211–278). Asimov's running commentary reflects his ambivalent, occasionally hostile, feelings about his Jewishness (for example, "I'm all in favor of Jewish girls marrying gentile boys ... because why should the Jewish boys have all the bad luck," p. 222), but he is a wonderful storyteller, and in general, this is a great collection.

Ausubel, Nathan. *A Treasury of Jewish Folklore: The Stories, Traditions, Legends, Humor, Wisdom and Folk Songs of the Jewish People.* New York: Crown Publishers, 1948. Don't be misled by the title! In addition to including folklore, this is one of the great—perhaps the greatest—works on Jewish humor. Originally published in 1948, it is still in print. Oddly enough, a sequel volume produced by Ausubel, *A Treasury of Jewish Humor* (Garden City, New York: Doubleday, 1951), is not nearly as funny.

Avidor-Hacohen, Shmuel. *Touching Heaven Touching Earth: Hasidic Humor and Wit.* Tel Aviv: Sadan Publishing, 1976. Avidor-Hacohen, an Israeli rabbi, journalist, and scholar of Hasidism, has compiled many anecdotes and quotations not readily available elsewhere, particularly in the English-speaking world. Here you will find Rabbi Naftali's assessment of a well-known liar: "Not only is what he says untrue, but even the opposite of what he says is untrue" (p. 78); and Rabbi Yechiel's lesson from one of his teachers: "Never worry about two things—what can be corrected and what cannot be corrected. What can be corrected, should be corrected at once, without any worry. And as for what cannot be corrected, worrying will not help" (p. 108).

Bane, C., and Alan Dundes. *You Call This Living? A Collection of East European Political Jokes.* Athens, Ga.: University of Georgia Press, 1990; see chapter 9, "Always the Jews," pp. 160–168. Bane and Dundes annotate several hundred jokes, then compare other versions that appear in different collections.

Bermant, Chaim. *What's the Joke? A Study of Jewish Humor Through the Ages.* London: Weidenfeld and Nicolson, 1986. More historical than hysterical, Bermant's book is an overview of what Jews have laughed at throughout the ages. The author is widely regarded as perhaps the most perceptive observer of English-Jewish life.

Cohen, John, ed. *The Essential Lenny Bruce.* New York: Ballantine Books, 1967. See, in particular, the chapters "Jews" and "Religions Inc.: Catholicism, Christ and Moses, and the Lone Ranger."

Cohen, Sarah Blacher, ed. *Jewish Wry: Essays on Jewish Humor.* Bloomington: Indiana University Press, 1987. See, in particular, Cohen's introductory chapter, "The Varieties of Jewish Humor" and Irving Howe's "The Nature of Jewish Laughter."

Cowan, Lore and Maurice. *The Wit of the Jews.* Nashville, Tenn.: Aurora Publishers, 1970. A largely unknown but very fine compilation of witty comments and jokes by and about Jews. Here you will find German-Jewish philosopher Hermann Cohen's critique of Jew-haters: "An anti-semite may prove 'logically' that Jesus never existed, and may yet prove 'historically' that the Jews had him crucified"; Jack Benny's complaint: "If this isn't a Stradivarius, I've been robbed of a hundred and ten dollars"; and Berlin artist Max Libermann's annoyed comment to a woman who was chattering as he painted her: "Another word from you, and I paint you as you are."

Davies, Christie. *Ethnic Humor Around the World.* Bloomington: Indiana University Press, 1990. Davies's book is a scholarly and comprehensive tome that examines how some groups become the butts of very specific sorts of ethnic jokes.

Draitser, Emil, compiler and ed., and Joe Pariser, trans. *Forbidden Laughter: Soviet Underground Jokes.* Los Angeles: The Almanac Publishing Co., 1978.

Dudden, Arthur Power, ed. *American Humor.* New York: Oxford University Press, 1987. See Joseph Boskin and Joseph Dorinson's chapter on "Ethnic Humor: Subversion and Survival," pp. 97–117.

Dundes, Alan. *Cracking Jokes: Studies of Sick Humor Cycles and Stereotypes.* Berkeley, Calif.: Ten Speed Press, 1986. Dundes, an anthropologist and folklorist at the University of California-Berkeley, deals with the kind of jokes my book has generally ignored: those that are hostile and virulently antisemitic. Yet, his study of the dark side of humor is important, for, as the author warns, "Don't be deceived by the facade of humor. People joke only about what is most serious." The book's specifically Jewish material is found in chapter 3, "Auschwitz Jokes"; chapter 6, "The Jewish American Princess and the Jewish American Mother in American Jokelore"; and chapter 9, "The Jew and the Polack in the United States: A Study of Ethnic Slurs."

Dworken, Leo. *Is Your Dog Jewish?* Philadelphia: Running Press, 1989. This Jewish version of Gregory Stock's surprise best-seller, *The Book of Questions,* is a half-serious, half-humorous compilation of 199 questions intended to arouse animated discussions. Some examples: "How do you feel about Jews who have cosmetic surgery to look less Jewish? . . . If you were given $50,000 to write an enthusiastic blurb for the jacket of a book by Yasir Arafat, would you do it? . . . Who's the worst *yenta* you know? What's the worst story he or she ever told you?"

Eilbirt, Henry. *What Is a Jewish Joke? An Excursion into Jewish Humor.* Northvale, N.J.: Jason Aronson, 1991.

Eliezer, Ben. *The World's Best Jewish Jokes.* London: Angus and Robertson Publishers, 1984. Eliezer has also written a sequel, *More of the World's Best Jewish Jokes* (London: Angus and Robertson Publishers, 1985).

Freud, Sigmund. *Jokes and Their Relation to the Unconscious.* New York: Norton, 1963. The first systematic study of the psychological underpinnings of jokes, Freud's book contains much Jewish material, almost all in Section A, chapters 2 and 3, "The Technique of Jokes" and "The Purposes of Jokes."

Goldman, Albert. "Boy-man, Schlemiel; the Jewish Element in American Humor," in Murray Mindlin with Chaim Bermant, eds. *Explorations: An Annual on Jewish Themes.* Chicago: Quadrangle Books, 1968, pp. 3–17.

Harris, David, and Izrail Rabinovich. *The Jokes of Oppression: The Humor of Soviet Jews.* Northvale, N.J.: Jason Aronson, 1988.

Hochstein, Peter, drawings by Sandy Hoffman. *Up from Seltzer: A Handy Guide to Four Jewish Generations.* New York: Workman Publishing, 1981. Each section of this book of cartoons focuses on how Jewish mores have changed during the past four generations in America. For example:

> *The Official Causes of Death:*
> *First generation—"He worked himself to death so you could have a better life."*
> *Second generation—"When he heard you flunked out of medical school, he died of a broken heart."*
> *Third generation—"I warned him not to play tennis after a big lunch."*
> *Fourth generation—"He blissed out on Quaaludes."*

Katz, Molly. *Jewish as a Second Language: How to Worry, How to Interrupt, How to Say the Opposite of What You Mean.* New York: Workman Publishing, 1991. Some Jews might be offended by Katz's stated purpose in writing this book: to help gentiles married to Jews understand their particular—and sometimes peculiar—ways of thinking and speaking. One of the disadvantages of marrying into a Jewish family, Katz notes, is that "you'll never have a brother-in-law who can replace your voltage regulator." On the other hand, "you won't have to look at tattoos," and "your spouse won't die of cirrhosis." She also warns gentiles, her husband included, against trying for total accuracy when they incorporate Yiddish words into their conversation: "We love to hear you deliver howlers like, 'When she found out she wasn't invited, she made such a big *shmatta* you could hear her down the street,' or 'Put everything on my bagel—nova, onions, the whole *shlemiel*.'" (*Shmatta* means "rag"; the speaker may have meant *shrei* (cry); *shlemiel* means "fool" or "ne'er-do-well," while *shmeer* may have been intended.)

Kertzer, Morris. *Tell Me Rabbi.* New York: Collier Books, 1978. These memoirs of a distinguished pulpit rabbi recount humorous episodes from both his life and those of other well-known Jews. A popular speaker at countless, and endless, Jewish meetings and banquets, Kertzer recalls Eddie Cantor who, when he was introduced after fourteen previous dinner speakers, began: "My dear friends, when I came here, I was a young man." He mentions a trauma that befell the great Jewish essayist and lecturer Maurice Samuel. "In Johannesburg, South Africa, he was introduced to a large gathering only a few hours after he had emerged from an arduous prop-plane flight from Europe. The chairman, Rabbi Rome, spent over forty minutes in a wearying introduction. [Samuel] rose, and in a withering voice declared; 'Ladies and gentlemen, while Rome was fiddling, I was burning.'"

Knox, Israel. "The Traditional Roots of Jewish Humor." *Judaism,* 12 (1964–1965), pp. 327–333.
———. "The Wise Men of Helm." *Judaism,* 29 (Spring 1980), pp. 185–196.

Kogos, Fred. *1001 Yiddish Proverbs: A Storehouse of Folk-wit and Wisdom from the Jewish Past and Present.* Secaucus, N.J.: The Citadel Press, 1974.

Kumove, Shirley. *Words Like Arrows: A Treasury of Yiddish Folk Sayings.* New York: Schocken Books, 1985.

Lukes, Steven, and Itzhak Galnoor. *No Laughing Matter: A Collection of Political Jokes.* London: Penguin Books, 1985. This book contains more *Jewish* humor than the title might lead one to expect; there are also jokes here that I have not seen in other collections.

Maccoby, Hyam. *The Day God Laughed: Sayings, Fables, and Entertainments of the Jewish Sages.* New York: St. Martin's Press, 1978. All of Maccoby's several hundred selections are drawn from the Talmud, making this book unlike any other collection of Jewish humor. His choices and comments deeply influenced my chapter on the Talmud and Jewish humor.

Marks, Alfred. *I've Taken a Page in the Bible: A Medley of Jewish Humor*. London: Robson Books, 1985. A British collection that contains some jokes I have not found elsewhere. The author is a wonderful storyteller. For example:

> *Two young rabbis, rivals for a pulpit in a European city, were asked for interviews. They arrived the night before and stayed in adjoining rooms of a local hotel. One of the candidates, Berman, had written out a sermon to deliver the next day, and he practiced it remorselessly throughout the night, reading it out loud time after time.*
>
> *The second candidate, however, whose name was Abelson, had [neglected] to prepare anything and he went to bed early.*
>
> *When the morning came, the elders of the community called the applicants in alphabetical order.*
>
> *Abelson was summoned and proceeded to deliver the sermon he had heard repeated so many times the night before in the next room.*
>
> *Now poor Berman heard this, but when his turn finally came, he had no choice except to repeat the same talk which he had prepared the previous night.*
>
> *The interview panel hurriedly met in closed sessions and after some discussion a decision was reached: If a man could hear a sermon once and then repeat it word for word he must have a remarkable [mind], they said. And so Berman was elected rabbi.*

Mason, Jackie. *How to Talk Jewish*. New York: St. Martin's Press, 1990.

———. *Jackie Mason's 'The World According to Me!'* New York: Simon and Schuster, 1987. This contains the text of Mason's phenomenally successful Broadway comedy act. Most critics regard his monologues on the differences between Jews and gentiles as the funniest part of his show.

———, with Ken Gross. *Jackie, Oy! Jackie Mason from Birth to Rebirth*. Boston: Little, Brown, 1988).

Mendelsohn, S. Felix. *The Jew Laughs*. Chicago: L. M. Stein, 1935. A collection of Jewish jokes. Mendelsohn published a second collection, *Let Laughter Ring* (Philadelphia: Jewish Publication Society), in 1941. These two books contain many of the classic stories exemplifying Eastern European Jewish humor.

A disturbing feature in these otherwise valuable collections is a periodic misogyny so pronounced that one wonders at the author's reason for including such jokes. In one story, Breine asks her husband Selig, "Just because you claim to be so wise, do you know the day I am going to die?"

"I certainly do," the husband replies. "You are going to die on the eve of a holiday."

"How do you know that?"

"It's simple. I know that the day following your death will be a holiday for me" (p. 102). Jokes like these might well have been the forerunner of the anti-Jewish women "JAP jokes" that began circulating in the 1970s.

Mindess, Harvey, Ph.D. *The Chosen People? A Testament, Both Old and New, to the Therapeutic Power of Jewish Wit and Humor*. Los Angeles: Nash Publishing, 1972. A psychologist's perceptive examination of Jewish humor.

Mr. "P," *The World's Best Yiddish Dirty Jokes*. New York: Castle, 1984. Reprinted by special permission of Citadel Press.

Novak, William, and Moshe Waldoks, eds. and annotators. *The Big Book of Jewish Humor*. New York: Harper and Row, 1981. A classic work, and probably the largest-selling volume ever written on Jewish humor, this book is a gold mine. Unlike all other books, it contains, besides jokes, many cartoons, short stories, excerpts from *Mad* magazine, and much more.
———. *The Big Book of New American Humor*. New York: HarperCollins, 1990. The book contains some Jewish material, the funniest, in my opinion, coming from comedian Jonathan Katz: "I had dinner with my father last night, and I made a classic Freudian slip. I meant to say, 'Please pass the salt,' but it came out, 'You prick, you ruined my childhood'" (p. 70).

Olsvanger, Immanuel. *Royte Pomerantsen: Jewish Folk Humor Gathered and Edited*. New York: Schocken Books, 1947. 249 selections of Jewish humor and folklore. Before you run out to try to acquire a copy of this out-of-print book, be aware that it is written in Yiddish in English letters. However, it does contain a very perceptive English-language introduction.

Oring, Elliot. *The Jokes of Sigmund Freud: A Study in Humor and Jewish Identity*. Philadelphia: University of Pennsylvania Press, 1984. Among the more interesting finds in this study of the first scientific writer on Jewish humor is this comment by Ernest Jones, Freud's disciple and biographer: "A gentile would have said that Freud had few overt Jewish characteristics, a fondness for relating Jewish jokes and anecdotes being perhaps the most prominent one" (p. 2).

Pollack, Simon. *Jewish Wit for All Occasions*. New York: A and W Visual Library, 1979.

Rabinowitz, Rabbi H. R., compiler. *Kosher Humor*. Jerusalem: Rubin Mass, 1977.

Rosten, Leo. *Giant Book of Laughter*. New York: Crown, 1985. A listing of jokes by topic; the book has sections on Israel, Jews, and other similar subjects.

―――. *Hooray for Yiddish: A Book About English*. New York: Simon and Schuster, 1982.

―――. *The Joys of Yiddish*. New York: McGraw-Hill, 1968. One of several books Rosten has written on Jewish humor, this has become a classic and is one of the best works on the subject.

―――. *The Joys of Yinglish*. New York: McGraw-Hill, 1989. Rosten intersperses recollections of his intensely Jewish upbringing with jokes and linguistic anthropology.

―――. *People I Have Loved, Known or Admired*. New York: McGraw-Hill, 1970. See, in particular, the chapter on Groucho Marx, p. 59–75.

Ruksenas, Algis. *Is That You Laughing Comrade? The World's Best Russian (Underground) Jokes*. Secaucus, N.J.: Citadel Press, 1986.

Schoffman, Stuart. "What Makes Jews Laugh?" *Jerusalem Report,* November 8, 1990, pp. 46–49.

Shulman, Abraham. *Adventures of a Yiddish Lecturer*. New York: The Pilgrim Press, 1980. A recounting of journalist Abraham Shulman's experiences lecturing before Yiddish-speaking audiences throughout North America. Along the way, he imparts much helpful advice to speakers. For example: "The man to reckon with most is the chairman; he was put there not for your glory but for his own. Don't object when he compares you to Albert Einstein or Bertrand Russell, he doesn't mean that you are a mathematician or a philosopher, he is just announcing that he is aware of such names."

Singer, Joe, compiler. *How to Curse in Yiddish*. New York: Ballantine Books, 1977.

Spalding, Henry, compiler and ed. *Encyclopedia of Jewish Humor: From Biblical Times to the Modern Age*. New York: Jonathan David, 1969.

Triverton, Sanford, compiler. *Complete Book of Ethnic Jokes*. New York: Galahad Books, 1981. See Israeli jokes, pp. 197–212, and Jewish jokes, pp. 229–286.

Van Den Haag, Ernest. *The Jewish Mystique*. 2nd ed. New York: Stein and Day, 1977. A popular and highly perceptive psychological and sociological study of American Jewry. Chapter 4, "To Suffer Is to Survive—and Vice Versa," pp. 57–70, contains an analysis of Jewish humor.

Vorspan, Albert. *Start Worrying: Details to Follow: An Insider's Irreverent (But Loving) View of American-Jewish Life*. New York: UAHC Press, 1991. Vorspan, longtime director of the Commission on Social Action for Reform Judaism, has compiled biting, humorous, and highly accurate essays about American-Jewish life based on "forty years of Jewry duty."

Whitfield, Stephen. "The Distinctiveness of American Jewish Humor." *Modern Judaism*, 6:33, October 1986, pp. 245–260.

Wilde, Larry. *The Complete Book of Ethnic Humor*. Los Angeles: Pinnacle Books, 1978. See Jewish jokes, pp. 148–173.

————. *The Great Comedians Talk About Comedy*. New York: Citadel Press, 1968. Among the comics Wilde interviewed for this book are Woody Allen, Jack Benny, Shelley Berman, Joey Bishop, George Burns, and Jerry Lewis.

————. *The Last Official Jewish Joke Book*. New York: Bantam, 1980.

————. *More: The Official Jewish Joke Book*. Los Angeles: Pinnacle Books, 1979.

Wisse, Ruth. *The Shlemiel as Modern Hero*. Chicago: University of Chicago Press, 1971. An important work about Jewish humor and much more by one of the preeminent contemporary scholars of Jewish literature.

Youngman, Henny. *Henny Youngman's Giant Book of Jokes*. Secaucus, N.J.: Citadel Press, 1966. Jewish material is sprinkled throughout this collection by America's king of the one-liners.

————, with Neal Karlen. *Take My Life, Please!* New York: William Morrow, 1991. Youngman's Jewishness permeates his humor, as is readily apparent in this autobiography: "I was actually present," Youngman recalls, "at the invention of one of the most famous one-liners of all time. Woody Allen even used this joke in *Annie Hall* to explain his feelings about how awful life is, and yet how it all still ends too soon. Unfortunately, I didn't make this joke up—it came my way from an angry older Jewish woman complaining to me about the fare at the Swan Lake Inn. 'The food here is terrible,' she said to me. 'And such small portions!' A classic. In reply, I simply said, 'Madam, the food at the Swan Lake Inn is fit for a king. Here, King! Here, King!'" (pp. 109–110).

Ziv, Avner. *Personality and Sense of Humor*. New York: Springer Publishing Co., 1984.

Index

▶